NITISH ENGINEERING RECONSTRUCTING BIHAR

NITISH ENGINEERING
Reconstructing Bihar

Sanjay Sinha

KALPAZ

ISBN: 978-81-7835-977-9

Price : ₹ 490

First Published 2013

Published by

Kalpaz Publications
C-30, Satyawati Nagar,
Delhi - 110052
E-mail: kalpaz@hotmail.com Ph.: 9212142040

Laser Typesetting : Rajender Vashist, Delhi
Printed at : G. Print Process, Delhi

Cataloging in Publication Data--DK
Courtesy: D.K. Agencies (P) Ltd. <docinfo@dkagencies.com>

Sinha, Sanjay Kumar, 1966-
Nitish engineering : reconstructing Bihar / Sanjay Kumar Sinha.
p. cm.
Includes index.
ISBN 9788178359779

1. Nītiśa Kumāra, 1951- 2. Economic development--India--Bihar. 3. Bihar (India)--Economic policy--1991- 4. Bihar (India) --Politics and government--21st century. I. Title.

DDC 320.954123 23

Contents

THE DALAI LAMA

FOREWORD

The appearance of this book is timely. Since the present Chief Minister of Bihar, Nitish Kumar, took up this responsibility in 2005, significant progress has been made there in the important fields of health and education, infrastructural development and law and order. I have been visiting Bihar regularly over the years, since my first pilgrimage to the site of the Buddha's enlightenment in Bodh Gaya in 1956, and have observed the many changes that have taken place since then.

Nitish Kumar is also someone I have got to know quite well and I can attest to his dedication to improve the lot of the people of Bihar. Perhaps in the spirit of friendship he won't mind my retelling here what happened when he invited me to attend the inauguration of the Buddha Smriti Park in the state capital Patna a few years ago. The Chief Minister made a fine speech in which he expressed his conviction that, with the blessings of the Buddha, the state of Bihar would now prosper. When my turn came to speak, I suggested, half-jokingly, that if Bihar's prosperity depended only on the blessings of the Buddha, it really should have prospered a long time ago. After all, Bihar is home to the most sacred site for Buddhists - Bodh Gaya, where the Buddha attained full enlightenment. For real change, we require more than the blessings of the Buddha, powerful though they may be. We also need action, which will only come about through the able efforts of the Chief Minister and others like him.

Nitish Kumar is not only a man of ideals, but someone who takes action and tries to put them into practical effect. Not content with the symbolic value of having transformed the site of a prison in Patna into the Buddha Memorial Park and built a great stupa there, he is taking steps to ensure that it also becomes a functioning centre of learning. I share with him the conviction that education is the means for engineering far reaching improvements in our world.

April 8, 2013

Preface

Though writing about the situation in a state does not attract attention of people living outside it. But the turnaround story of Bihar is no ordinary narration of story. Its transformation from time a decade back as "jungle raj" to the one prevailing now has drawn positive response from within the country as well outside. The story of Bihar is talked about widely in the political and social circle.

The book "Nitish Engineering: Reconstructuring Bihar" has tried to bring the truth of the story from horses mouth (common citizens). Though the issue is politically volatile as opposition parties strongly dispute any claim of development in the Ntiish Kumar rule but political talks apart commonman thinks otherwise. The author has tried to paint the right picture of the state by talking to people from cross section of the society in different parts of the state.

The book deals with the background over seven years ago when law and order was the source of all news originating from Bihar. The state and its people had become a subject of ridicule and hatred in the country.

The advantage with the author is that he has seen both the world (one that existed for 15 years and lasted with coming into power of the present rule of Nitish Kumar in November 2005 and the one after that). The good and bad experience gathered during the period made the task of drawing a true picture of the state easy.

The story of change has been told through micro study of places of eminence and what people residing there thinks of comparative times. The author interacted with people in far off places of Jiradei (birth place of First President Desratna Rajendra Prasad), Sitabdiara (native place of JP), Motihari (from where Mahatama Gandhi had launched his satyagrah against British rule) and a number of other places to understand the mood of the people earlier and now.

It incorporates positive soundbites the state is drawing now. From Tibetan spiritual leader and noble prize winner the Dalai Lama to many diplomats and foreign dignatories have praised the change they saw in Bihar and wished it well to make rapid strides on the path of development. They all acknowledge perceptible change in situation in the state than and now.

The man responsible for the change is nobody else than Chief Minister Nitish Kumar who through his hard labour and positive mindset has written happy story of Bihar. His image in the country has risen substantially due to his painstaking efforts to transform Bihar. The book narrates the difficult times he passed through and some interesting facts and stories of the person.

The story would be incomplete if it talks only about present and does not highlight the future of the state. The last chapter through the heading challenges ahead highlights the major challenges lying before the Chief Minister and the state to keep up the present pace of growth. The 2014 general elections is considered as a major watermark for Bihar as it would decide whether the ruling combination continues as it is today and continue writing bright history of the state or the development comes to a grinding halt due to break up of relationship and a new political journey of the state.

Sanjay Sinha

Acknowledgements

For an experienced person, writing a book might not be a big deal. But, for the first timer like me the adventure was onerous and full of challenges. But, as the work progressed, nervousness turned into excitement. The things went right mostly because of support of family, friends and colleagues.

My wife Priti Sinha and children Shashank Sinha and Tabishi Sinha stood like rock with me all along and would render help whenever I needed it.

The thought of writing the book cropped up during one of the visit to a noted Astrologer Amar Gautam at Shimla (where I was posted as State Bureau chief of PTI from 2007 to April 2010), who said after seeing my horoscope that time was ripe for me to write a book.

Though initially I treated it lightly, but my wife grabbed the words and had been after me ever since which forced me to try hand at penning a true story about changes taking place on the field in Bihar.

My elder brother Sharat Kumar Sinha, who is a senior officer with Delhi Police, Bhabi Rina Sinha, niece Shilpi Shreya and Shefali Priya, eldest Bhabi Ruby Sinha and nephews Nishant Sinha and Prashant Jayant showed eagerness about the book from the beginning to end which fuelled energy in me.

The project could not have taken wings without the support and encouragement of Editor-in-Chief of PTI, Mr M.K. Razdan. His interest and knowledge of the subject boosted my confidence. Whenever he got anything on Bihar, he would pass it to me.

Besides, he would regularly ask me about the going ons in Bihar and discuss the points and counterpoints about growth story of the state.

I received help from my PTI colleagues in various districts of Bihar who accompanied me to the field in the interior areas.

Many interesting piece of information was gathered from recent writing of Arun Sinha, a close friend of Chief Minister Nitish Kumar.

Filmstar–politician Shatrughan Sinha, who is Lok Sabha member from my native place Patna Saheb, has been a perennial source of inspiration. Whenever I felt the task is tough and dithered, he would say "*Khamosh!*."

Sanjay Sinha

Introduction

Bicycle riding boys and girls clogging traffic in cities, women beauty parlours flourishing in small villages of Dumri Bujurg, Seetalpur and Nayagaon in Sonepur (from where Rabri Devi, former Chief Minister and wife of RJD President Lalu Prasad lost assembly elections in 2010), large number of outlets providing e-tickets of Railways and Airlines at relatively small places like Dighwara near Chhapra are enough to reflect that Bihar has said goodbye to its old image of being a 'dark' place in the last nearly two decades and transformed itself into a promising happening place now.

Ending days of darkness that had made lives of people miserable across the state since 1989 till half-a-decade back when kidnapping for ransom and *rangdari* (extortion) tax from businessmen and professionals were routine things in Patna and other places, Bihar no longer grabs national media front page for poor law and order and crime situations.

By effectively checking crimes like kidnapping and *rangdari*, the "fear factor" has vanished from the mind of people on the large and they could be seen roaming freely with families even late in the night in Patna and other cities.

There was a time when extremely worried mothers used to pray to the almighty for safe return of their husband and children from offices and school/colleges, but this is a sad and deadly story of the non-productive past. Now, happy families are seen shopping, taking dinner at restaurants and enjoying joy rides on the widened roads in Patna and other towns late in night. Life has become pleasant and comfortable for citizens.

This is Bihar of present much better them nearly a one-and-a-half decade of non-rule since 1989, (when Lalu Prasad's RJD had assumed rein of Bihar igniting peoples hope in the name of social justice.

As part of speedy trials, more than 65,000 people were convicted in the state between January 2006 and December 2011. Of those convicted, more than 150 were sentenced to death while 1,224 got life terms and 3,124 were sentenced to more than 10 years of jail. Under Bihar's Special Courts Act, 2011 that empowered authorities to confiscate a public servant personal property even during trial; the government to amusement and honesty seized properties of such six officer including those of an IAS and an IPS, and converted those consfications into schools for underprivileged.

The transformation is more lucid in district Siwan, the birth place of the First President of independent India Dr Rajendra Prasad, where for sheer misfortunes citizens of late were forced subjected to live under the bayonet of RJD strongman and former MP Mohammad Shahabuddin. With the strongman caged (he is convicted to life sentence by a special court of district Siwan in a criminal case) and police becoming hyper active, citizens seem to have forgotten the F (fear) word.

People could be seen walking around in Siwan town till late in the night, something they could have never imagined over half-a-decade back. Now possible which and not with Cross-section interactions of people in Siwan reveal that there was literally no life after sunset earlier. Returning home safe after after marriage parties or some other social functions after sunset was unthinkable. Some of them remember how daughters and sisters were taken away forcibly by goons from Railway stations after alighting from trains late in the evening, or while waiting to catch a train.

Citizens of Jiradei, a community development block some 15 km from district headquarters where lies the home of Dr Rajendra Prasad and which is also home to Mohammad Shahabuddin, say the "fear factor" no more bother them, as goons are either behind the bars or have fled out of fear of police.

Glee has also returned on the faces of natives of Sitab Diara, the birth place of Loknayak Jaiprakash Narayan in neighbouring Saran district and Motihari, the district headquarters of East Champaran from where Mahatama Gandhi had launched 'Champaran' satyagraha by organising protest against forceful cultivation of indigo by the Britishers in 1917.

Natives of JP's village, situated on the bank of river Saryu about 130 km from capital Patna, are particularly happy that now there is no instance of theft of their cattle which worried them in the inglorious past.

Free movement of peoples in Bhagalpur town, which had seen a massive communal riot in 1989, is a common sight as also in the case of famous tourist destinations of Rajgir, Darbhanga and Motihari.

With establishment of peace by tightening the law and order situation, the state is working hard to oil the rusted government machinery.

Bihar recorded an overall growth rate of 16.71 per cent during fiscal year 2011-12, the highest in the past five years. Bihar recorded 10.7 per cent growth rate at constant price in 11th five year plan (2007-12) highest in the country. The enhanced growth rate of 10.79 per cent in the 12th five year plan has been possible because of record production of food grains. Other sectors that have driven growth are construction, hospitalities and telecommunications.

Bihar's roads, agriculture, food and social welfare are witnessing spurt of activities. The timely action and efficient handling of situation helped Bihar minimise the Agro-damage due to poor monsoon in 2012. Sensing trouble as early as May-June 2012, the Bihar government that faced rainfall deficiency in between 20-32 per cent, had announced diesel subsidy and 5-8 hours of uninterrupted power supply in rural areas to protect standing crops. Such measures were announced at the national level as late as in August when sowing areas of major kharif crops had already dwindled by nearly 5 lacs hectares.

The official records say that Bihar is receiving more foreign tourists now a days than Goa, considered a tourists, to be paradise. According to statistics, nearly 70 lacs foreign tourists visited India in 2011 out of which 9.7 lacs came to Bihar alone, much higher than the footfalls in Goa, blessed with voters who compared him for the doings of his RJD rule for an inauspicious strech of 15 years in the state scenic beauty and beaches.

Mukhyamantri Balika Cycle Scheme is creating waves across the country. With over 20 lacs students of standard IXth are given cycle to have a facility to attend to schools in the last four years, the dropout rate in schools has come down to 3.5 per cent now from a higher of 12 per cent earlier. As a result of the scheme, 97 per cent of all girls now attend schools.

Major streets being jammed by bicycle riding students by school hours is a eye soothing scene to watch in Motihari, Rajgir, Araria, Saran and other places, too.

Distribution of free uniform to girl students of classes IX, X, XI and XII under Mukhyamantri Balika Poshak Yojna under which Rs 1000 per student is distributed for school dress is also working wonder, in driving students to schools.

Roads are also drawing praises for Bihar, where people used to grumble travelling on the potholed roads, but now love driving on long routes.

Former chief minister Mr. Lalu Prasad Yadav had failed to deliver on his promise to make roads of Bihar so smooth as to be compared with the cheeks of the film actresses Hema Malini, but Nitish Raj has certainly made road journey a pleasant experience for masses.

The government promises to reduce travel time from remotest part of the state to Patna to under six hours. Except for a far-off district Kisanganj, the said target has been almost achieved by the state government.

With around 1.7 lacs km roads built or redone in the last six years in Bihar, State Road Secretary Pratya Amrit says the claim is not empty.

During last five years, Bihar Rajya Pul Nirman Nigam (BRPNN) has delivered 645 bridges at a cost of Rs 2,025 crore. The state's road density has gone up to 126.13 km from 111 km mark of 2008. Total road length has increased by 20 per cent in the last year to 1.13 lacs km.

The big achievement found voice in famous International magazine "Economist", which said, "world class overbridges, gleaning roads and new automobiles are fast becoming Bihar's identity."

Prestigious US-based "Time" magazine reecently in one of its issue carried a story titled as "How One Man Cleaned up the Dirtiest State". Inside the magazine, the credite report reads about 'How Nitish Kumar turned Bihar into a model of Indian reform'.

On the path of regaining its past glory, Bihar is attracting accolades from famous personalities, both at home and from abroad.

"The situation in Bihar has improved considerably. Positive initiatives and leadership has led to these changes," said Noble Laureate and Economist Shri Amartya Sen.

"This is not the Bihar of old. Now schemes and roads are visible. Immunisation against dangerous diseases has shown progress," said Microsoft giant Bill Gates who is associated with campaign against Polio.

"I am very happy to be in Bihar. The work of Nitish Kumar is quite encouraging," said the Tibetan spiritual leader His Majesty the Dalai Lama who visited to inaugurate Budha Smriti park in 2010 at Patna, which has come up on the ruins of old jail building.

A World Bank report said, "Chief Minister's efforts to give Bihar a special identity have been acknowledged. To start business, Patna is better than Mumbai."

More recently, United Kingdom Finance Minister George Osbrone showed eagerness to explore opportunities for British companies to invest in Bihar.

"Bihar is on the move...Bihar has emerged as an inspiring model of positive change and good governance. Bihari society in general and its youths in particular appear eager to create new opportunities for economic growth and development," said US Under Secretary of State for Political Affairs Mr. Wendy R Sherman, who paid a diplomatic visit to Patna in April 2012.

Reflections of Bihar's growth could be seen in drastic drop in percentage of migration of labourers from Bihar to Punjab, Surat and Delhi. According to a survey done by Bihar Economic Growth Institute, there has been around 26 per cent fall in migration of labourers to outside from Bihar in 2009. This is attributed to maximum developmental works being undertaken in the state which are creating employment to them apart from the Centre sponsored MGNREGA scheme which assures 100 days of employment to the willing.

A state Labour department estimates showed migration of labourers from Bihar in search of livelihood to Punjab, Gujarat, Maharashtra and Delhi has declined by almost 30 per cent. State Labour Minister Mr. Janardan Singh Sigriwal said, a fresh labour survey has been ordered particularly in districts like Araria, Purnea, Saharsa and Kisanganj which witnessed large-scale migration movement of labourers to outside states. Preliminary reports emanating from the survey carried jointly by state Labour Department officials with those from A N Sinha Institute of Social Studies and NGOs, suggest the percentage has dropped further. Mr. Sigriwal says, this has happened because of large-scale development works being carried out in infrastructure sector like building of roads, bridges and hospitals which is keeping labourers engaged at home itself.

The fact is not merely confined to books, but pangs of shortage of labour keep pouring from Punjab, the cradle of Green Revolution of 70s.

Bicycle manufacturers of Ludhiana and big farmers of Punjab are offering free mobile set and bicycle to Bihari labourers to retain them to work. With the labour shortage not improving despite all freebies, the cycle manufacturers fear their age-old profession of bicycle manufacturing is in danger. Many of the units engaged in manufacturing bicycle unable to cope up with the situation have downed the shutters while the rest are continuing with a lot of hardship.

The man credited with bringing this turnaround is none other than Chief Minister Shri Nitish Kumar. Ever since he took rein of Bihar in November 2005, Kumar, a product of JP movement of 1974, has not spared even a minute in bringing development to the state. Today he is referred to as the CEO (Chief Executive Officer) of Bihar.

Son of a freedom fighter Ramlakhan Kaviraj from Kalyanbigha in Bakhtiyarpur, on rural outskirts of Patna, Nitish Kumar is known for his no-nonsense attitude.

Into his second inning, the 62 year old Bihar CM is also known by the titles like "Vikas purush" and "Sushasan Kumar" because of good governance.

Heading JD(U)-BJP coalition government in the state, Kumar is strongly opposed to "Pariwarvad" (dynastic politics). He is a stickler to rules and in his long political career spanning over three decades, never a finger has been raised at him for corruption. The display of high standard of integrity and honesty helped him earn trust of peoples who were fed up with the naked display of power by the de facto first family of the state in the past and "salas" (brothers-in-law) of the strongman (Lalu Prasad) of Bihar for a long time.

In the midst of all these development talks, masses are also comparing Nitish with Lalu Prasad. Majority view is that Lalu who enjoyed absolute power in Bihar for nearly 15 years missed the opportunity to change the face of the state which Nitish did through sincere efforts. People view that Mr. Lalu fiddled when Rome was burning but Nitish through his hard work has successfully repaired the inherited damages timely and ushered the state on the path of development, a high matter to enlist the accolates reporoted from everywhere.

Nitish also proved Lalu wrong that elections can not be won on the principle of *vikas* (development). The thumping victory of JD(U)-BJP rule for the second time in 2010 under leadership of Nitish was observed due to honest work of the state leadership. Forced politically, Lalu also raised development issues during the polls but it did not cut much ice with the voters who capered him for the doings of his

RJD rule for a starch of 15 years in the state since inauspicious 1989.

Though a new environment conducive to growth has been created in Bihar, critics feel the present trend of development is not sustainable. Planning Commission member Abhijit Sen had recently described growth pattern of Bihar as "nursery or catchment area growth."

Noted Industrialist Kumar Mangalam Birla during Bihar Global Summit in February 2012 at Patna asked Bihar to improve its power supply position to attract industries to the state.

The concerns raised by him is not untrue. With an annual generation capacity of a little over 300 MW against requirement of 5000 MW, electricity is a scarce commodity in the state. With power consumption of 75 kwh (kilowatt per hour) per capita, Bihar lags behind even Gurgaon, a sattelite city of Delhi having power consumption of 1,265 kwh. The average at national level is 600 kwh.

Bihar has been seeking special package from the Centre to rebuild itself after carving out of mineral-rich Jharkhand state from it in 2000. Chief Minister Nitish Kumar has made strong pitch for special category status for Bihar by tweaking norms. His party JD (U) organised "Adhikar rally" at Patna and Delhi's Ramlila Maidan. The special status issue has become a major agenda for 2014 general elections in Bihar.

Chief Minister led an all-party delegation to Prime Minister Manmohan Singh seeking 50 per cent power allocation from NTPC's two upcoming units at Barh in Patna district and Kahalgaon in Bhagalpur district and coal linkages for two new units of 250 MW each coming up at Barauni.

Extending helping hand, the Union government has agreed to allocate 50 per cent power supply from Barh stage-II.

Due to all these efforts, Bihar registered the highest Decadal Literacy Award by the President of India.

Though Bihar is sprinting on the path of development, but a big challenge lies about how long the ruling coalition partners would go together. News reports indicate that if BJP, the coalition partner of JD (U) in Bihar, pushes the case of Gujarat Chief Minister Narendra Modi for Prime Ministership in 2014 General Elections, it would be but a bit difficult for Nitish Kumar to continue the ties with the saffron party.

Nitish in an interview to a newspaper had categorically said that the NDA Prime Ministerial candidate should have "secular" credentials. A statement which was seen as his strong protest to candidature of the Gujarat leader carrying tint of 2002 communal riots in the western state and who is seen fast expanding his reach out of the state. The Bihar CM, who is a senior leader of Janata Dal (United), second largest constituent of NDA with 29 MPs, had told Ex-BJP President Nitin Gadkari to ensure that Modi is not chosen as PM nominee.

RSS Chief Mohan Bhagwat's statement that in terms of governance Bihar was better than Gujarat, had triggered another round of Modi versus Nitish debate. When asked to comment on Sarsanghchalak of RSS, the ideological guardian of the BJP, polite Nitish said he believed in doing his work sincerely and did not like to be compared with anyone.

Nitish as PM gained currency recently when a Bihar minister Bhim Singh asked the BJP to name Nitish Kumar as NDA nominec for the post in 2014 Parliamentary polls to honour sentiments of people of Bihar. But, the minister's view was not appreciated by the patient and non-impolite Chief Minister himself who later on reprimanded him following which the minister, who once was a close supporter of Lalu Prasad before joining JD(U) on the eve of 2010 Assembly elections, ate his words and regretted for his act. While, Nitish silenced the minister fearing it might smell bad that he was building up a case for himself the Deputy Chief Minister of Bihar and BJP's most prominent face in the coalition government Sushil Kumar Modi jumped on the bandwagon saying Nitish was a Prime Ministerial material and he should be given an important role in the 2014 general elections.

Though the numbers do not support his candidature for the PM post, political pundits opine that in the case of hung Parliament, Nitish with clean image and solid support among muslims might be supported by either of the two national parties—Congress and BJP. They point out the case of H D Deve Gowda and I K Gujral and say in any case Nitish has much wider acceptance than them across the country.

In the midst of political turmoil at the Centre recently triggered by resignation of Trinamool Congress (TMC) on the issue of hike in diesel price and allowing 51 per cent FDI in multi-brand retail, Nitish turned the pot further hot by tossing an issue that the 40 Lok Sabha MPs of Bihar would matter a lot in the formation of a government at Delhi after 2014 general elections.

He said his party would extend support to anyone in 2014 who promise to provide special status to Bihar to speed up its development. His assertion at Bettiah while addressing an "Adhikar rally" triggered speculation if Congress-led UPA would grab the opportunity. While this did not happen but the issue would hold a lot of importance in the 2014 Parliamentary elections in which JD(U) is expected to further improve its tally on the back of remarkable performance of Nitish government. The JD (U) has 29 MPs presently in both Houses of Parliament.

But in case Nitish falls out with the BJP on Narendra Modi issue and decides to do a Navin Patnaik, it's a matter of conjecture how strong his government would be without long term friend BJP. Numbers would not be a problem for him in such eventuality as his JD (U) has 117 MLAs in 243-member Bihar assembly where the magic figure is 122. With a large numbers of Independent and members of smaller parties waiting in the wings to support JD (U), mustering the required numbers would not be a tough task but, without support of BJP , the scenario might not be the same. On this count, the 2014 Parliamentary elections are crucial for Bihar and its future growth process.

1

Clearing Jungle Grown in Past 15 Years

- Once dismissed as a hopeless state due to poor law and order and dismal developmental record, Bihar is making rapid strides to regain its past glory.
- The journey to growth had a difficult background as the state was in shambles. A World Bank report on Bihar titled 'Bihar: towards a development strategy" painted a grim picture of the state.
- Tracing the state of affairs and performance since 1990, the report says that nearly 40 per cent of Bihar's population lives below the poverty line, the highest in India. Its poverty gap, which measures the depth of poverty is also far above the national average. Modest progress was made during the 1990s (1993-94 to 1999-2000), reducing poverty by 7 per cent, but the rate of poverty reduction was well below the national average.
- This has been accompanied by much slower progress than the rest of the country in meeting the Millennium Development Goals (MDG). By the current trends, Bihar is projected to fall well behind on the most of MDG targets for 2015 undermining the national performance, the report said.
- Bihar's growth which was slightly below national trend in the 1980s became far lower subsequently. The state experienced zero growth in the first half of 1990s. Since 2004-05 the growth has averaged 3.8 per cent or about 1

per cent per annum in per capita term. As a result, income growth and computation levels in Bihar have lagged seriously thereby widening gap between Bihar and the rest of the country. Underlying this result has been Bihar's exceptionally weak performance in agriculture and modest performance in service, the World Bank report said.

- The declining level of investment in Bihar has led to low growth performance. Private investment in the state has been exceptionally low as compared with other states and Bihar's share of private projects being implemented in the 1990s was lowest among major states. Public investment level have also been seen a downward trend partly due to state's fiscal constraint. Despite significant government's contribution to the growth, fiscal difficulty negated the desired results. The state's bifurcation in November 2000 exacerbated the fiscal outlook as the new state of Jharkhand received most of revenue-yielding and mineral resources while Bihar retained most of the liabilities. Bihar's fiscal crisis was evident in deteriorating road quality, dilapidated schools, health clinics with no medicine and very low level of rural electrification.
- Programmes resources allocated to Bihar from the Centre are also not being fully utilised even though the state is more dependent on these transfers to finance public investment and development schemes than other states.
- Bihar had the country's lowest utilisation rate for centrally funded programmes and it is estimated that the state forfeited one-fifth of central plan assistance during 1997-2000.
- Social service delivery reflected by lack of education, poor health, inadequate safe drinking water and sanitation was bad during the period. Only 10 per cent of the children were fully immunised in 2000.
- Bihar has many poverty alleviation programmes to improve livelihood of the poor and socially disadvantaged virtually all of them funded by the Centre, there performance appears to be quite weak in general mainly due to mis-targetting of funds and institutional difficulties in using government fund efficiently.

- Evidence of mis-targetting could be gauged from the fact that Public Distribution System (PDS), Bihar's most important social safety net programme, reveals that under coverage (the qualified poor households which do not receive the food subsidy) totalled 89 per cent in 1990-2000 and leakage (the non-qualifiying families receiving benefits) being 46 per cent during the period.
- The report gave some selected indicators for Bihar and India to highlight the situation. While poverty headcount at national level was 28.6 per cent in 1999, it was 39 per cent in Bihar. Likewise prevalence of child nutrition/ underweight children below 5 years of age was 47 per cent at national level while it was 54.4 per cent in Bihar. Access to improved sanitation referring to household with toilet facility was 36 per cent at national level but it was less than half than this at 16.8 per cent in Bihar. Households with electricity on as source of lighting was 55.8 per cent at All India level but was absymally low at 10.3 per cent in Bihar, the report highlighted.
- Such was the difficult background from which Nitish Kumar started the efforts to bring the state on the path of development. Seeking to rise virtually from the ashes, Bihar's growth story is abound with significant works being carried out in different fields like education, health, roads, agriculture and social welfare, particularly for minority muslim community which compriseS around 12 per cent of the state's population.
- An honest attempt is underway in the past six years to remove thickly accumulated rust from the government machinery and oiling them to deliver faster results.
- Though the government has launched new schemes in all the departments, innovative attempts in some sectors like roads, education, health and law and order have earned it kudos from people not only of the state but also outside.
- A brief reference of works in these fields considered as core sector would be helpful in understanding the changes taking place in the state.

Law and Order situation

- The crime situation prior to 2005 was so bad that the state had earned the tag of jungle raj. Kidnapping and *rangdari* (extortion) had taken the shape of an easy and volumptuous industry. Broad day light robberies, chain snatching had become common events. Women were deprived of their gold chains while waiting for their children at the school bus stops in Patna. Once a woman was robbed of her golden chain from her neck while purchasing vegetables outside her home at 6 am in the morning in a colony in the heart of the state capital.
- Several PILs were filed in the Patna High Court against the spate of kidnapping for ransom and extortion from businessmen and professionals like doctors and engineers. Several doctors and school children had fallen in the trap of kidnappers.
- Doctors, engineers and school children had launched several protests against abduction of their fellow colleagues. Organising *yagnas*, special prayers and marching on the streets were a common sight in the state capital. It appeared these had become part of students extra curricular activities.
- Kidnapping hatched by criminals from inside the jails were frequently reported by newspapers then, which also highlighted on several occasions how ransom money used to reach jails for purchase of freedom for abducted. Scorpios and Boleroes used for kidnapping had become ugly things as they were seen by people as vehicles of crime.
- Noted filmmaker Prakash Jha showed the modus operandi of kidnapping by different gangs in his movie "Apaharan" starring Ajay Devgun and Nana Patekar. His another film "Gangajal" which also came around that time attracted people because of name of the villain as "Sadhu Yadav" which drew uncanny similarity to the name of infamous brother-in-law of Lalu Prasad. The movie could be released in the theatres of Bihar only after Jha convinced Prasad that it had nothing to do with character of his controversial brother-in-law.

- Though kidnapping of doctors and schools children were almost a daily event in Patna and other prominent cities, a few incidents stirred the conscience of the entire nation. thanks to media, both print as well electronic.
- Kidnapping of prominent doctors – Dr Ramesh Chandra and Dr Bharat Singh had led Indian Medical Association (IMA) Bihar chapter hit the streets.
- Abduction of class VII student Golu by dragging him inside a car at busy Bailey road after pushing aside his grandfather at school bus stop had shocked the nation.
- Kidnapping of an official of NHAI (National Highway Authority of India) from Muzaffarpur while working on a road project had shaken the confidence of people from outside the state to work in the troubled state. Murder of IIT graduate Satyendra Dubey in Gaya, who had blown whistle at corruption in building of golden quardilateral road project, had hogged the limelight. The matter was ultimately handed over to CBI for investigation.
- While the administration had become a mute spectator to public woes, the criminals raised their stock after being frequently named in news reports for kidnapping and extortion. Criminals used to dispute for the use of adjectives for their rivals like "history-sheeter", "dreaded" and "Terror of Taal (riverine belt)" etc. which they complained unnecessarily lifted their reputation in the world of crimes.
- While the entire state was burning in the fire of kidnapping and extortion, Siwan witnessed a parallel government of former RJD MP Mohammad Shahabuddin. The period showed the cold-blooded murder of JNU student leader Chandrasekhar in the heart of Siwan. A Special Court had convicted Shahabuddin and his three shooters to life imprisonment in 2009 in the same case. The conviction disqualified him from contesting the last General Elections. The poll saw defeat of Shahabuddin's wife Heena in the hands of an Independent Om Prakash Yadav who was supported by ruling JD(U). It is said that earlier, rival candidates of Shahabuddin used to campaign outside the confines of Siwan out of fear of the [RJD] strongman.

- The former MP is also facing trial in several other cases of kidnapping and murder of CPI-ML workers and assaulting policemen. Two policemen were killed in a fierce encounter between the men in khaki and Shahabuddin at his native Pratappur village where they had gone to raid his house.
- News poured over in the newspapers and TV channels as how Lalu Prasad's two powerful brothers-in-law —Sadhu Yadav and Subhas Yadav played godfather to many criminals. There were frequent news of Lalu Prasad's nephew Nagendra Rai donning the role of a terror for shopkeepers and real estate people in Raza Bazar area in western Patna.
- Almost all the towns of Bihar were flooded with strongmen enjoying patronage of powerfuls in Patna at that time.
- Inheriting the state in such an explosive condition, the biggest challenge for Nitish Kumar, who had come to power riding on the hopes of people to get rid of "misrule" of RJD in 2005, was to clean the jungle.
- Mursilessly cracking whips on the criminals, the Nitish government is today praised for establishing rule of law. The situation could be better understood through comparative crime statistics (2001 to September 2011):

Year	*Murder*	*Dacoiety*	*Theft*	*Kidna-pping*	*Highway robbery*	*Dacoiety*
2001	3619	1293	2175	385	1296	22
2002	3634	1259	2236	396	1323	28
2003	3652	1203	2425	335	1430	14
2004	3861	1297	2909	411	1875	30
2005	3423	1191	2379	251	1310	26
2006	3225	967	2138	194	1251	15
2007	2963	646	1729	89	1109	19
2008	3152	640	1536	66	897	16
2009	3152	654	1619	80	962	07
2010	3362	644	1538	72	1051	09
2011	2465	423	1034	42	747	06

(Till September 2011).

- Another indication of better law enforcement and improved internal security is evident from statistics of conviction of criminals (January 2006 till September 2011):

Year	*No of cases*	*Criminals convicted*		*Types of Sentence*		
	IPC	*Arms*	*Act*	*hanging*	*lifer*	*10 yr*
2006	2178	1156	6839	17	1389	366
2007	3695	800	9928	39	2168	680
2008	4461	706	11012	27	2307	610
2009	5333	482	13163	12	1824	375
2010	6201	427	14311	37	1875	640
2011	4128	259	9663	1	1365	435
(till Sept)						
Total	25996	3830	65916	133	10928	3106

- Various steps have been initiated to tighten law and order situation. The police manpower were boosted by recruitment of Special Auxiliary Police (SAP) comprising former army personnel. Three counter-insurgency and anti-terrorism (CIAT) schools came to be at Dumroan (Buxar), Bodh Gaya (Gaya) and Dehri-on- Sone (Rohtas) haste being,.
- Speedy trial of offenders connected with railway dacoiety, armed robbery and drugging of railway passengers. 1,180 offenders were sentenced till September 2011.
- Creation of 510 posts for the SC/ST police stations, being set up in 30 districts. Women police stations established in all 38 districts. A mega project of Rs. 106 crore for construction of police barracks, residences, police outposts and police lines have been approved for the police force.
- The state has launched a fight against corruption. Zero tolerance towards corruption is being diligently followed.
- Details of moveable and immovable properties of the Chief Minister, Ministers, bureaucrats and police servants (with the exception of class D employees) have been posted on the government website as part of exercise at transparency.
- For confiscation of disproportionate assets earned by public servants through corrupt means, six Special Courts have

been set up under Bihar Special Courts Act and Rules (two each in Patna, Muzaffarpur and Bhagalpur) in 2010.

- Addressing the corruption issue, a house and land seized on September 2011 of a former IAS officer S S Verma by the government has been converted into a primary school at Rukunpura Musahari in Patna. Another such property of a former state police chief Narayan Mishra has been converted in a school in the state capital. With these two, a total of six such confiscations has been done so far.
- Entrapment and catching of corrupt public servants red-handed are in progress. A total of 61 such traps is executed and 68 arrests made till September 2011. The annual average of such cases from 1996 to 2005 was only 4.5.
- The improved law and order situation has generated a soothing experience for people of Siwan. Citizens have almost forgotten the meaning of the word fear and could be seen roaming around in the town till midnight, a welcome scene from the days when life literally used to come to a standstill after sunset.
- The situation is best described by Krishna Prasad locally known by the name of "TT Babu" because of his retirement from Railway from the post of TT. A close associate of Dr Rajendra Prasad, TT Babu said, "people here no longer live in the shadow of guns and goons."
- While this was the view of people of the birth place of the First President of independent India, citizens of Sitab Diara, the native village of Loknayak Jaiprakash Narayan and Motihari from where Mahatma Gandhi had launched Indigo movement against Britishers in 1917 and which is also home to well known writer James Orwell are no less happy.
- Dilip Shrivastava, a native of Sitab Diara is particularly happy that there is no theft of cattle now.
- Sharing experience of Motihari, Ranvijay Singh, former Bihar minister said, now people do not hesitate to return to their homes from some social function even late in night.

- Many family restaurants have come up in Motihari in view of rush of families came out for outings which was not possibie earlier.

2. Roads

- Another major things that is catching imagination of people is betterment of roads in the state. The state government has achieved the target of making journey from any remotest part of the state to Patna within six hours. Secretary, Road Construction Department, Pratya Amrit proudly claims they have nearly achieved the target. Chief Minister Nitish Kumar says except for far-off Kisanganj district, the road journey from any district headquarters to Patna could be achieved within six hours.
- Government statistics reveal that during last six years, the Road Construction department has improved/upgraded 7087 km of Major District Roads (MDRs) at a cost of Rs. 4037 crore. Work is in progress on a further 1420 km.
- 643 km of National Highways have been upgraded to 4-lane and an additional 1065 km are to be upgraded to 2-lane with paved shoulders. An additional 745 km are to be improved under Special Projects (World Bank funded). A 95 km strech of NH-82 and 127 kms of NH-83 have been proposed for upgradation to 4-lane standard at a cost of Rs. 4143 crore with financial assistance from JICA (Japan International Cooperation Agency).
- All old state highways (2035 kms) are being made 2-lanced under Rashtriya Sam Vikas Yojna at a cost of Rs. 2979.92 crore by central agencies (CPWD and IRCON). Till date about 1950 km have been completed. 2747 new State Highways have been declared of which 82 km are being made 2-laned with Asian Development Bank (ADB) assistance. Till date 520 km of the project has been completed.
- Improvement of 2132 km of National Highways from state plan has been repeorted. There are 28 NHs passing through Bihar whose length is 3734 km.

- Physical achievement of Road Construction department in financial year 2006-07 to 2011-12 are as follow.

Financial Year	*Km completed*	*Amount (in crores)*
2006-07	983	Rs 704.15
2007-08	1913	Rs 1210.18
2008-09	3106.26	Rs 1544.135
2009-10	3473.88	Rs 1899.998
2010-11	2890.36	Rs 3310.278
2011-12	956.30	Rs 2555.79
Total	13322.80	Rs 11224.531

- For all the five districts identified by the Central government as naxal-hit including Gaya, Jehanabad Aurangabad, Arwal and Jamui, an approval has been given for upgradation of 677.71 km of roads there (606.88 km under MDR and 70.83 km of NHs) at a cost of Rs. 616.335 crore in the first phase. Against this till February 2012 work has been completed on 308.27 km. Target has been set to complete work on the rest by March 2013.
- Goverrnment of India has decided to construct a 2-lane road along Indo-Nepal border. Road Construction Department of Bihar has been declared executive agency for this project within the state which totals to 557 km. The work is likely to be completed in 2014-15.
- Besides roads, the government has also worked on bridges to reduce journey time. The bridge work has been done through Bihar Rajya Pul Nirman Nigam (BRPNN), a sick state PSU till 2005. During last five years the corporation has built 645 bridges at a cost of Rs. 2025 crore.
- In addition, several mega bridges have also been constructed prominent among which are 354 metre Kataunjha over river. Bagmati, 600 metre Dubbaghat over Bagmati, 579 metre long Jhaua over Mahananda, 579 metre long Lava over Mahananda and 456 metre long Larjha over Kareh.

- Mukhya Mantri Setu Nirman Yojna, is a scheme which envisages construction of small and medium bridges with a view to provide year-round connectivity in rural areas. Over the last five years Rs. 2500 crore have been provided under the scheme wherein 3119 of the 4655 bridges taken up have been completed.
- Roads and bridges have brought about a turnaround in the lives of people in far-flung areas. The test case is Bairgania, the last nagar panchayat of India on the Nepal border. There is a *tenous* rail link between Bairgania and the rest of world. But for several months in the year, when the river is in flow if they miss the train or if tracks are flooded, the people of this small hamlet are stranded.

  To get to the hospital in the district headquarter of Sitamarhi or beyond it to Muzaffarpur or Patna they have to take a time consuming and often perilous route. First, the road or the lurching dirty track that passes for it up to the river, then the boat and again the road.

  To mitigate peoples, woes, the government has approved a 600-metre long bridge over Bagmati in the nearby village of Dheng. The bridge promises to connect India to its nagar panchayat even in the condition when the water rises.
- Anjana Shrivastava of Humayunpur village of Sitamarhi is happy because now she could reach her village within half-an-hour from Sitamarhi railway station because of metallic road upto her village. She recounts that earlier they had to walk or take bullockcart to reach home after ardous journey of over four hours.
- Shafalta Singh and her husband Rakesh Kumar are jubiliant because they could drive down to their village in Paliganj block from the state capital within an hour thanks to smooth road upto their doors in the village, which has considerable influence of maoists.
- Road construction work, which earlier used to be a bone of contention between major criminal gangs ruling a particular area has been made transparent by making provision for e-tendering for works above Rs. 25 lacs.

- In addition to computerisation of all works divisions including headquarters, on-line toll free helpline (18003456161) has been installed at the headquarters.
- Several flyovers in the state capital has helped mitigate traffic jams.
- Sanjay Pandey of Motihari said earlier roads were in such a bad shape in the town that cars needed frequent servicing. One can reach any block of East Champaran from the district headquarters in less than half-an-hour, he said. Sikandar, a taxi driver, said journey to Biharsharif from Patna was a difficult proposition earlier because of potholed roads but now on thick metallic road driving there is hillarious and cut shorts time substantially.

Health

- One of the important areas which is earning good name for the state is health which majority concerns the comman man.
- Once feared as "death trap" due to unhygenic condition and poor service delivery, the new-look of government hospitals are increasingly winning faiths of the people as manifested by nearly 100 per cent jump in footfalls in these institutions.
- Official statistics show that in 2006 only 39 patients used to visit primary health centres (PHCs) in a month which has risen to 3500 to 5000 patients per month now. In 2010-11 nearly 4 crore patients got treatment in government hospitals. The same soared to 4.86 crore till December in the fiscal 2011-12.
- In 2007-08 only 7.98 lacs of people registered themselves with hospitals in the state which jumped to 24 lacs in 2010-11 and to 31.2 lacs till December in 2011-12 financial year.
- Infant mortality rate, maternal mortality ratio and total fertility rate are continously decreasing in the state.
- Considering seriousness of the problem of malnutrition and child health, the government has launched "Muskan scheme". Nutritional Rehabilitation centre has been

established in 32 districts so far to provide nutrition and treatment to severely malnourished children as well as nutrition and hygiene education to mothers.

- The state has earned a distinction in prevention of Vitamin A deficiency in 95 per cent of children wherein the national average is 34 per cent. Similarly, vaccinations for different diseases have seen an overall increase. This is the reason why Bill Gates applauded Bihar as a leader in immunisation at the World Health Assembly in Geneva in 2011.
- The increase in institutional births is another good indicator. The state has recorded a six-fold increase from 2005 to 2011 in this respect.
- All the block level health Centres being made functional for 24 hours. Due to implementation of intensified polio eradication programme, only 9 cases of polio were found in 2010 while no cases of polio detected in Bihar from September 2010 to October 2011.
- Process has been initiated to upgrade all primary health institutions to 30 bedded health centres by making Bihar medical services and infrastructure corporations fully functional.
- Under grievance redressal system, 1911 telephone service of health department can now be accessed through SMS (9711981981) and online www.statehealthsocietybihar.org.
- There has been increased trend of institutional deliveries in the state as manifested from the fact that while in 2006-07 institutional delivery was only 4 per cent which rose to astronomically high of 51 per cent in 2011-12.
- In 2010-11, family planning accorded priority, 5.16 lacs of family planning operations were done as compared to only one lacs in 2005.
- The population stabilisation programme has been strengthened under public private partnership. Fertility rate is currently 3.9 in Bihar. In 2010-11, 5.16 lacs family planning operations were done and 3.45 lacs females provided with copper-T, contraceptive pills, emergency contraceptive pill and condoms sold through ASHAs in 36 districts at sub-divisional and district hospitals.

- Special programme has been launched for school children for their health check-up, distribution of child health card and provision has been made to make available vitamin A and deworming medication once in 3 months under Nai Pidhi Swasthya Gaurantee Programme.
- Steps have been taken for expansion of basic health infrastructure. There were 8,858 health sub-centres in 2004-05. Based on population, decision has been taken for construction of 7,765 new health sub-centres. Funds released for construction of 2,350 health sub-centres against which 767 are completed.
- In 2004-05, total number of Additional Primary Health Centres (APHC) was 1,243. Based on population a decision was taken to construct 1,544 new APHCs. Funds have been released for building 217 APHCs.
- 180 sample collection centres and 27 pathological testing centres have been established at PHCs, FRUs and SDHs under PPP mode. Similarly, radiology centre (X-ray, ultrasound) have also been set up under PPP mode. Till now 293 x-ray centres and 34 ultrasound centres have been set up. 3,09,554 X-ray, 38,737 ultrasound and 10,46,558 pathological tests have been done free of cost from January 1st, 2011 to 31st August, 2011.
- Much to the glee of poors, the government hospitals down to PHCs levels are providing 13 pathological tests including those of blood sugar, biopsy, *lipid* profile, SGPT, urea and urine (sugar) free of cost.
- For other costly tests the rates are highly subsidised. As per the rates fixed, Rs. 25 is charged for creatinine test and Rs. 15 for platelet count.
- The much improved functioning of the government hospitals are driving people towards them from far and wide. Increased footfalls at government hospitals have harmed private practices of doctors in Patna and other places.
- The standard of the government hospitals could be seen from a visit to any such centre even in remotest part of the state.

- It was around 9 o'clock in the night. While the entire Bhagalpur town was in dark due to load shedding, the 30-bedded Sadar hospital was fully lighted by two generators.
- Two doctors, half a dozen nurses and an assistant staff were on duty.
- The tiles fitted surfaces and lavoratories were clean and no stinck came from any quarter as used to be an usual scenario earlier in any government hospital in the state when people had to negotiate with the dirty smell by covering their nose with handkerchief.
- Despite being late evening, the hospital was streamed by a large number of people which reflected their growing faith in government hospitals.
- One side of the hospital is reserved for nutritional rehabilitation of malnourished children aged in between 6 month to 5 year. 20 children are selected from one block who are feeded with nutritional food for 21 days along with their mother to make them healthy.
- A beaming Pawan Kumar said this hospital is very old, and never in the past such a high standard has been maintained because of which people used to hesitate to go there. But, now the scenario is totally different...this hospital is rushed by people from far and wide throughout the day.
- The scene at Primary Health Centre, Sabour in the same Bhagalpur was also an eye-opener. Hundreds of people particularly women were jostling with each other to reach to the doctor and receive free medicine, Lathi-wielding policemen were seen fighting to maintain a proper queque of the milling crowd.
- Built in 1908, PHC Sabour which caters to the need of nearby 110 villages in an area of 144 km, is receiving over 500 patients daily, officials said.
- An old hand in the hospital who took me around the PHC said, in his over 30 years of posting in the hospital built by the Britishers, he had never seen more than a handful of patients descending there earlier.

- The PHC which used to carry child-births under a dim light of 40 watt bulb and with only one set of equipment, has five beds with separate equipment sets and powerful halogen hanging overhead now.
- HIV kits are properly stored in a cold box which is provided to pregnant women to test both mother and baby of the dreaded disease.
- The PHC has elaborate pathological facilities.
- The state's premier Patna Medical College and Hospital (PMCH), where only those who did not had the money to go to private nursing home, used to go, is now a hot favourite of the poor and as well as to do.
- "Due to improved service delivery at PMCH and other government hospitals, peoples, dependence on private nursing homes have come down," said S N Mishra, Head of Cardiology Department at PMCH.
- He said against 50-60 patients daily, the footfalls in the cardiology wing of the hospital is as high as 300 people everyday nowow.
- The scenario at PHC Rivilganj in Saran district of the state was also pleasing.
- Looking after the needs of nine panchayats and a population base of nearly 1.25 lacs, PHC Rivilganj has 24-hour emergency facility.
- Three regular and four doctors appointed on contractual basis are on regular duty. There is no dearth of medicines as the supply comes without delay from civil hospital Chapra, Dr Dhananjay Kumar Sinha, the head of the PHC, said.
- Despite located at an isolated place, the PHC is visited by more than 150 people daily which had never been the case earlier.
- Attached to the PHC is an Additional PHC in nearby Sitab Diara, the birth place of Loknayak Jaiprakash Narayan. Though there is no emergency provision there, it provided medicine for common diseases and against snake bites a common danger in the area.

- Much to the comfort of citizens, similar is the scenario at government hospitals be it Nalanda, Motihari or Darbhanga.

Education

- Once known as a seat of learning, that state's common education system in Lalu Prasad Yadav's much celebrated years in the post Independence Indian history had touched nadir. Late running of academic sessions, murderous and deficient upkeep of schools and colleges had left nothing for the luckless students but to rue their fate.
- Over half-a-decade back, there was not much talk on revival of education system but Lalu's emphasis was laid on opening "Charwaha Vidayalaya" (school for shephards) and "Pahalwan vidyalaya" (school for wrestlers). Though the concept of such institutions was not bad as it aimed at educating the poor engaged in family business of cattle rearing from very childhood, but as the newspapers that report clearly it was a political popular *gibe* aimed at appeasing a helpless section of society towards the power that was. The schools which started with much fanfare remained in a very poor condition and not much could be achieved out of them.
- With ascendency to the power, Chief Minister Nitish Kumar made his priority very clear that his thrust would be to encourage citizens to fill ink in pen in place of *oiling the lathis*, the slogan given by his predecessor.
- Working on the age old saying that ideas are mightier than swords, the new dispensation gave a big push to revamping the education system. Several schemes were launched to enthuse thoroughly the students as well as schools and colleges, all sats of for learning.
- The most important scheme among them which continues to win laurels for the Nitish Raj has been providing bicycle to boys and girls of class IX in government schools across the state. The "Mukhyamantri Balak cycle scheme" and "Mukhyamantri Balika cycle scheme" have been making waves across the country and many states have borrowed

the idea from Bihar to cut down school dropout rates in there places.

- Launched in 2008, the yojna is working wonders for th as due to such efforts to mainstream the non-enrolled children. their number has decreased from 12 per cent to 3.5 per cent.
- According to government record, out of a physical target of distributing 6,25,256 cycles among boys in different districts in 2010-11 a total of 5,69,523 cycles were handed over to the beneficiaries in that year. The government achieved 91 per cent of the target it had set under the programme for boys all the districts.
- The achievements were 100 per cent in Araria, Arwal, Gaya, Katihar, Madhubani, Purnia, Sheikhpura, West Champaran and Siwan.
- The achievement was slightly better for girls as the state government achieved 92 per cent of the physical target it had set for distribution of cycle for girls as per the scheme for them. Out of the target of 5,32,497 'a total of 4,89,446' cycles were provided to the girls under the programme.
- The success rate was 100 per cent in Araria, Arwal, Bhojpur, Buxar, Jamui, Kishanganj, Lakhisarai, Madhepura, Madhubani, Purnia, Saran and West Champaran.
- The bicycle riding students clogging the traffic of main streets of the cities during school hours are a pleasant experience. The scene of bicycle riding students particularly the girls is a photographer delight. A separate shed for parking bicycles in the school is overcrowded with the "*dupahia*" (as the bicycle is known in this part of the country).
- During a visit to the famous tourist spot of Rajgir in Nalanda district, I saw girls in genuine earnestness rushing on their bicycle to schools. Similar soothing scenes could be seen in Saran, Siwan, Kishanganj, Motihari and Bhagalpur.
- Dr Farooq Ali, a lecturer in famous TNB College and General Secretary of four schools run which he for students of minority communities in Bhagalpur, said the cycle

scheme has boosted attendance in Muslim High School, Urdu Girls High School and CMS High School.

- But, the flip side of this much talked about scheme is that there has been complaints reported of fake registration of students for lust of bicycle and also registering a student at more than one place. However the CM has ordered an inquiry into such complaints.
- At remarkable success of Nitish bicycle scheme, his rival Lalu Prasad recently announced providing bus to nearly 60 schools out of his MPLAD fund in his Chapra parliamentary constituency. The effort is seen as his attempt to counter bicycle with bus. The RJD boss is veering round the the same idea to repeat (providing bus to schools) in the three other constituencies held by his part men in the state.
- Alongwith the bicycle scheme it is another ambitious programme to provide the students with school uniform. The Mukhyamantri Poshk Yojna is equally popular.
- Under the programme provision of cash grant for school uniform is allowed to the children studying in classes I to VIII at the rate of Rs. 400 per student for classes I and II, Rs. 500 for classes III, IV and V and Rs. 700 per student for classes VI, VII and VIII.
- Now under Mukhyamantri Balika Poshak Yojna, girl students of classes IX, X, XI and XII are provided Rs. 1000 per student for uniforms. Twenty lacs girl students had benefited from the scheme in 2011-12 financial year.
- As a result of all these efforts, Bihar registered the highest increase in general literacy at 16.82 per cent and female literacy at 20.21 per cent in the country and was conferred Decadal Literacy Award.
- Many other efforts are underway to perk up education system in the state.
- To improve quality of elementary education, a new programme "Samjhen-Sikhen" has been started in all 71,000 elementary schools.
- Lok Shiksha Kendra has been established in each panchayat. At these kendras, the neo-literates would do

reading-writing and cultural activities. Shaksharata Kendra were started on November 11, 2011.

- For web based online monitoring and management software for successful implementation, effective management, monitoring and evaluation of mid-day meal scheme a registered society was constituted for these purposes.
- 370 industrial training centres were established in the private sector. In 2011-12 five new Industrial Training Institutes were sanctioned. All 38 districts of the state have now been covered with industrial training facility.
- To motivate students, Dr Rajendra Prasad Merit Scholarship Award has been instituted for the toppers of the secondary school examinations from 2011. The state topper received Rs. 15,000 and a laptop worth Rs. 35,000 with data card. The second to 10th rank holders received Rs. 10,000 and a laptop with data card. Toppers of each of the three streams for the higher secondary examination received a prize of Rs. 15,000 and a laptop with data card.
- For developing the capabilities of teachers, training via video-conferencing is introduced with the help of Edusat satellite and CIET, New Delhi.
- Under Mukhyamantri Balika Protsahan Yojna, an incentive of Rs. 10,000 is being granted to SC/ST and extremely backward community students who secure first division in the secondary school board examination. In 2011, 10,013 SC students and 1,243 ST students benefitted. From extremely backward classes, 33,405 students received incentive.
- For welfare of minority muslim community, a Rs. 43 crore scheme for the modernisation of madarsas was approved. All madarsas were provided with academic calender 2011-12 from Bihar State Madarsa Education Board.
- The state government is resorting to different ways and means to improve education system. An encouraging effort in this direction was celebration of 'Shiksha Rakhi'. To ensure children's right to education through enrolment in schools, the state government in association with Bihar Education Project (BEP) newly launched a unique initiative

named 'Shiksha Rakhi' on the day of Raksha Bandhan on August 2012. As part of the initiative school-going children tied rakhis on the wrist of out-of-school children and inspired them to enroll themselves in schools. The programme was inaugurated by District Magistrate of Patna who tied rakhi on the writs of a 14-year-old girl with "School Aao" (come to school) on it.

- UNICEF Bihar chief Dr Yameen Mazumdar in his address on the inauguration ceremony said it a novel effort. He went on to say it was heartening to see the enthusiasm of children in tying 'Shiksha Rakhi' to out-of-school children.
- Official figures suggest that 51,108 children are out of school in Patna district alone, while the figure for Bihar is 2,83,000. Thus Patna alone is contributing 16 per cent of the out of school children in the state.
- A new chapter would be written in the history of Bihar when Nalanda International University would start functioning.
- Noble prize winner economist Prof Amartya Sen has been appointed the Chancellor of the new university, which is an attempt to realive the old Nalanda university, which was seat of learning for the world in ancient times. Former President Smt. Pratibha Devi Singh Patil had earlier sanctioned the appointment of the Chancellor.
- The decision to appoint Mr. Sen as Chancellor of the Nalanda International University was taken at a meeting of the governing body of the university encluding the former Singapore foreign minister George Yeo as its member. Lord Meghnad Desai is also a member of the board.
- Chief Minister Nitish Kumar has demanded the opening of a school of economics and basic science at Nalanda University.
- The board decides that the process of recruitment of acclaimed and renowned faculties for the university begins in July 2013 and the academic session of its two schools—historic sciences and environment and ecology—starts from April 2014.

- The University, in Nalanda district, about 100 km from the state capital Patna, will be fully residential like the old Nalanda University. It will offer courses in natural sciences, philosphy and spiritualism along with social sciences.
- Mr. Kumar suggests the university has seven proposed vidyapeeths such as school of economics and management. He further suggests university remain under Union External Affairs Ministry and not with Union Human Resources Development (HRD).
- The university got a leg up recently when Yale University, Chicago expressed readiness to assist the university. The Ministry of External Affairs talks with the Yale to mentor its department of Environment.
- Bihar got a boost with the Centre approving two Universities for the state at Motihari and Gaya, due to persistent efforts of the Chief Minister. Nitish had persistently demanded location of the Central Univeristy at Motihari linked with Mahatma Gandhi. The Union Human Resources Development ministry under Kapil Sibal which had earlier turned down the state's demand and decided to open the university at Gaya a convenient location, agreed to Mr. Nitish's demand ultimately and approved an university each at Motihari and Gaya. This is the second instance the Centre agree to open collectively two central universities in a state. In past such educational policy decision was acknowledged for Jammu and Kashmir in year?
- Not satisfied with the naming of the university at Motihari as Central University North Bihar, Mr. Nitish shot off a letter to Sibal demanding the Centre to name it after Mahatma Gandhi as Motihari had been his "karambhoomi".
- Bihar has hogged the limelight also because of astounding success of Super 30.
- Super 30, a educational programme started by educationist Anand Kumar in Patna in 2002 under the banner of 'Ramanujan School of Mathematics' created high waves across the country and abroad. The programme selects 30 meritorious and talented candidates through entrance

examination every year specifically from Economically backward sections of society and trains them for the IIT-JEE, the entrance test for prestigious Indian Institute of Technology (IIT). The students hailing from humble background are provided free lodging and food and trained rigorously to crack IIT. Director General of Police of Bihar Mr. Abhyanand, himself an IIT graduate, taught physics to the students. Failed to pursue his dream to study at Cambridge due to acute financial problems, Mr. Anand took to Super 30 to help excel poor students. Many of the successful students are wards of truck drivers, daily wage earners or a peon.

- The unbelievable success of Super 30 has made it more then a famous name attracting accolades from more famous personalities. Bollywood icon Mr. Amitabh Bachhan acknowledged Anand's contribution in the making of the film 'Aarakshan'.
- Prestigious Time magazine recognised Super 30 in its list of Best of Asia 2010. The Super 30 received appreciation from American President Barak Obama's special envoy Rashad Hussain, who termed it the "best" institute of the country.
- Discovery Channel made an hour-long documentary on Anand's pioneering work, while Al Jazeera, Japanese Channel NHK, France 24 and various other channels made short films on Super 30.
- After impressing the Japanese, it has now attracted South Korea. A famous South Korean publishing company 'Amo Agency' has expressed desire to publish a book on Super 30. A South Korean magazine 'Cine21' ascertained Anand to be as popular in India as film stars.
- One of the films on Anand won the viewers choice award in the South Asian film festival in Los Angeles a couple of years ago.
- Chief Minister Nitish Kumar has on a number of occasions praised the noble effort of Mr. Anand in bringing children from marginalised section of the society at higher positions. Himself an Engineering graduate, the Super 30 gives a special happiness to the CM.

Agriculture

- Agriculture is the backbone of Bihar's economy. About 77 per cent of the state population is dependent on agriculture and related work in the state. Agriculture and Animal Husbandry contributes 18 per cent of the Bihar's GDP whereas, it is 16 per cent at the national level. Out of 93.60 lacs hectare area of the state, 72.96 lacs hectare is under agriculture. Farming is being carried in all the three agri-seasons—kharif, rabi and summers. Rice, wheat, coarse cereals and pulses are the main foodgrain crops produced in the state.
- Mr. Nitish Kumar time and again has said that his dream is that he wish to see at least one dish in every plate of an Indian out of agricultural produce in Bihar?
- Due to effective implementation of the centre sponsored Bringing Green Revolution in Eastern States (BGRES) special project, Bihar has increased its production of paddy to record 80 lacs tonnes in 2011-12.
- To give priority to agriculture sector, an Agriculture Cabinet developed of 17 different departments related to agriculture. The untired state government is further preparing "Agriculture Road Map" (2012-20 22).
- The state has prepared an agriculture roadmap for five years for the 12th plan at an estimated cost of Rs. 150 lacs crore, first experiment of its kind in the country. Target is to ensure at least 7 per cent growth of agriculture every year through effective implementation of the roadmap, says Mangala Rai, Agriculture advisor of the CM.
- The roadmap would work through coordinated efforts of 18 departments related to farm sector. No other state has such an integrated approach to agriculture.
- President Pranab Mukherjee launched the state's agriculture roadmap on October 3, 2012.
- International conference on Organic Bihar was Organised on 22-24 June, 2011 in Patna. Brand name "Jai B" was launched to give an identity to the organic agricultural products of Bihar.
- To increase foodgrain production and productivity, "Sri Kranti" was launched on January 27, 2011 from Patna.

Hybrid paddy cultivation was started in 4,03,000 hectare.

- To enhance soil fertility, free distribution of one lacs quintal seeds of Dhaincha was distributed to be used as green manure. Among the farmers Dhaincha was cultivated on 3.70 lacs hectare. Planting material of different horticultural crops was distributed among farmers viz— banana (11,12,800), Drumstick (3,60,000), mango (2,52,000), Litchi (33,880), Guava (26,5100) and Amla (68,970).
- To promote use of modern agricultural implements, Krishi mela were organised at every district level. 2,020 power tillers, 1,924 tractors, 16,227 pump sets, 5,417 irrigation pipe, 26 combine harvesters, 6,333 sprinklers and 76,967 canonweeders, a total of 1,29,362 agriculture implements, involving a subsidy of Rs. 73.67 crore were distributed.
- Soil testing campaign were conducted from 20-25 April 2011. Five soil samples were collected from each village. A total of 2,07,000 soil samples were collected and tested.
- In view of paucity of rains during kharif a diesel subsidy programme involving Rs. 369 crore was started. Diesel subsidy for two irrigation per one acre of land were sanctioned to all farmers. A subsidy of Rs. 20 per litre of diesel subject to a maximum of 10 litres of diesel were sanctioned.
- Bihar Shatabdi Niji Nalkup Yojna was started to sink 12,000 shallow tube wells in Samastipur and Nalanda districts. A lum sum bank loan of Rs. 12,000 to farmers, is not obligatory in this scheme.
- As a result of greater thrust being given to agriculture and related activities, Bihar farmers have achieved many milestones in recent times.
- Darbeshpura village in Nalanda which is also native district of Chief Minister Mr. Nitish Kumar, has been in the news recently for creating world record in production of paddy and potato.
- Union Agriculture minister Sharad Pawar had recently told Parliament about Darbeshpura village surpassing the Chinese record of paddy production.
- He quoted the state government report saying the yield of wet paddy has been recorded at 22.4 tonnes per hectare

and that of dry paddy at 20.16 tonnes a hectare. It has surpassed the yield of 19 tonnes per hectare which was recorded earlier in China.

- The record yield was achieved under demonstration on system of rice intensification (SRI) which was organised at farmers, fields during kharif 2011. The central government has been providing financial assistance of Rs. 3,000 for organising demonstration of 0.4 hectare each on SRI under national food security mission (NFSM-Rice) in identified districts of 16 states. This has been extended to Bihar and other Eastern states under the sub-scheme "Bringing Green Revolution in Eastern India" of Rashtriya Krishi Vikas Yojna (RKVY).
- Similarly a farmer of the same village who is nameshake of the Chief Minister made international record in potato. Farmer named Nitish Kumar managed to raise 729 quintal of potatoes applying organic farming techniques. The previous world record was registered in the name of Netherlands for producing 45 tonnes per hectare. Bihar is the third largest producer of potato in the country after Uttar Pradesh and West Bengal.
- Citing these achievements, Chief Minister Mr. Nitish Kumar has expressed confidence that his dream of da enegaed in organic fandaa second green revolution could be attained in a short span of time.
- Farmers of Nalanda engaged in growing organic vegetables received a shot in the arm recently with the despatch of first consignment of vegetables to Mumbai for further trading to Saudi Arabia and Russia. Nalanda Organic Vegetables Growers Association has signed an agreement with Delhi-based potato exporting firm Indian Potatoes Limited for shipping the staple veggie to Russia.
- Many experimental projects are being carried in by Bihar Agriculture University Sabour in Bhagalpur district. Built in 1908 by Britishers, the institution was accorded the status of an agriculture university in 2009.
- Farm scientists of the university are encouraging cultivation of strawberry in and around Bhagalpur. The

stone fruit, which hitherto was a preserve of hill states of Himachal Pradesh and Jammu and Kashmir, has shown encouraging results in the newer place of Bihar. Senior Scientist Rubi Rani said they are planning to distribute over 50,000 saplings of strawberry in 2012-13 to transform it as a commercially beneficial produce for the farmers of the region.

- Efforts have been made to streamline Animal husbandry and fisheries.
- A Rs. 3,200 per hectare annual premium for Fisheries Insurance Scheme, under which 50 per cent is contributed by the state government, is in action in the state. A Memorandum of Understanding (MOU) has been signed in this regard with Oriental Insurance Company Limited.
- Rs. 6.89 crore has been earmarked for the backyard goat rearing scheme and backyard poultry rearing scheme for Scheduled Castes. Programme for 20 ambulatory vans equipped with latest technology and veterinary medicines as part of 20 mobile veterinary hospitals have been categorically.
- There is plan for establishment of 300 new primary veterinary hospitals in addition to existing primary veterinary hospitals. To promote goat rearing, 30 per cent bank subsidy is provided to progressive farmers.
- Steps have been taken to boost milk and dairy items in the state, too.
- Bihar which was dependent on milk supply from Punjab and Andhra Pradesh to meet its domestic consumption is turning out to be a frontline state in milk production.
- From a low average milk procurement of 281.81 thousand litre per day in 1999-2000, the state is now obtaining nearly 14 lacs litre milk per day from farmers in 2011-12.
- Bihar is among first 10 leading milk producing states of the country, Ashok Java, General Manager of Comfed (Bihar State Cooperative Milk Producers Federation) said. Uttar Pradesh, Andhra Pradesh, Rajasthan, Gujarat, Madhya Pradesh, Maharashtra and Haryana are the major milk producing states of the country.

- The COMFED MD said that the state is targeting to procure about 32 lacs litres of milk per day by 2021-22 to further improve its ranking. Agriculture minister Narendra Singh attributed the success story to progressive approach of Nitish Kumar government.
- The state government is providing various incentives to the farmers, including subsidised feed and fodder and 30 per cent subsidy on purchase of animals among other things to promote milk output in the state.
- COMFED, which is the implementing agency of operation flood programme of dairy development on the pattern of Anand in Gujarat, MDsaid several steps are being taken to boost milk production in the state. These included technical inputs like providing breeding facility, animal health cover, food and fodder for keeping good health of livestock?
- Out of the 11 lacs litre of milk procured daily, the state is sending around 3.5 lacs litre of processed milk everyday to Mother Dairy, Amul and Delhi Milk Scheme (DMS) in the national capital and other states like Assam, Orrisa, West Bengal besides Nepal. A new dairy plant is coming up founded at Biharsharif for which the state government has allocated a fund of Rs. 121 crore.
- Bihar is fortunate in the sense that it is getting support from great scientist and former President APJ Abdul Kalam in giving a new thrust to farm sector.
- A technology mission in agriculture inspired by Kalam has worked wonders for farmers in remote Paliganj in Bihar with productivity of staple grains—rice and wheat—increasing by more than double.
- The mission run by Technology Information Forecasting and Assessment Council (TIFAC), a part of Ministry of Science and Technology under close supervision of Kalam has brought a turnaround in the economy of farmers in Paliganj block, around 25 km from Patna.
- The programme named 'Mission Mode Programme of Technology Vision 2020" was aimed at filling the technological gap for increasing crop productivity, TIFAC Director, Gautam Goswami, who looked after the mission

in Paliganj, said.

- Launched in 2000, the mission in Paliganj came to an end in 2011. But we still keep track of the things over there through different agencies, Goswami said.
- Narrating the success story of the programme, Goswami said prior to the mission, rice productivity in Paliganj was 2 tonne per hectare which has now risen to about 5 tonne a hectare. Likewise, of wheat the productivity was less than 2 tonne a hectare which has now jumped to 4-5 tonne a hectare.
- Kalam never forgets to mention about the success story of Paliganj in any function associated with agriculture and use of science in the farm sector.
- He said to provide better exposure to Paliganj farmers, he had organised four growers from there to visit Gujarat where agriculture is registering a growth of 9 per cent per annum. Similar trips were organised for Paliganj farmers to Amalsad Chikku fruit cooperative and Warana pura in Maharashtra where farmers can understand the merits of the cooperative system.
- Goswami said farmers were provided vital informations like, which crop to grow to maximise profit, how much fertilisers should be used and from where to purchase quality seeds.
- Hundred of farmers would be called at some community place like temple or panchayat bhawan and provided important information about affordable farm technology through which they could multiply their agricultural productivity, the TIFAC Director said.
- As a result of improvement in system and encouragement from the government, many enterpreuners have come forward to connect farm sector with latest technology.
- A shinning example of this is a topper student of prestigious IIM Ahmedabad Mr. Kaushlendra, who has developed ice-cooled push cart for selling fresh vegetables. The project is a hit in the state.
- Hailing from Nalanda district, which also happens to be the native district of the Chief Minister, Kaushlendra

dreams to make the vegetables the new brand of resurgent Bihar.

- After topping IIM-A, he did an extensive field study on agriculture by meeting farmers and closely watching cultivation techniques practised by growers before he gave of shape to his project. In a bid to establish direct contact with vegetable growers, he has tied up with over 250 vegetable growers in different villages in Nalanda and Patna districts.
- He also tied up with Agriculture Training and Management Agency (ATMA) to take his dream to vegetable producers in different parts of the state. As part of the programme, the NGO run by him purchases fresh vegetables from growers and keep, them in the ice-cooled box perched on push carts. The veggies which remains fresh for long time are sold to consumers. The project is visible in the state capital and his native Nalanda district where people are appreciating it. Recently, he launched the service in Lucknow where also he attracted encouraging response.
- The young entrepreuner, in his 20s, has now launched a prepaid card system for purchase of vegetables. The customers will be able to buy vegetables with the card even if they don't have cash, and also get them at a slighter lower price.
- The scheme which was started with on The push cart has?
- 300 farmers have associated themselves with the project?
- The government is encouraging agriculture through different farmer-friendly schemes to make farming a profitable occupation.
- Through "Naya Baag Lagao Abhiyan" plantations of mango, guava, banana and litchi have been extended in an area of 10,018 hectare. Farmer field schools have been established for providing weekly technical information to farmers by agriculture scientists and officers.
- The sick "Bihar Rajya Beej Nigam" has been revived seed production started in state and seed farms coming in vogue. There is a plan to establish e-kisan bhawan in each block. To enhance soil fertility, free distribution of one lacs quintal

seeds of Dhaincha has been planned as green manure. For development of horticulture crops plant materials of banana, mango, drumstick, litchi, guava and amlaare distributed among farmers.

- Facing almost 30 per cent rain deficiency in 2012, the government stepped into provide timely relief to farmers. A committee was formed comprising of Agriculture Advisor Mangala Rai, Agriculture Production Commissioner and Director Agriculture to assess the loss due to monsoon deficiency and to suggest alternative crops and provide them information of where abouts to buy seeds and market their produce.
- The government also ordered for providing 5-8 hours of uniterrupted power supply from its available capacity to rural areas to protect crops from damage due to shortage of rain water. Talking about bad monsoon, Mangala Rai said except for the five districts all others received lower amount of rainfall creating problem for agriculture and also hampering availability of drinking water and fodder.
- Bihar has launched a rainbow revolution for holistic development of an entire agro-based production system. The Eastern region with ample ground water has potential not only for cereals but also for pulses, vegetables, fruits, milk, fish and animal husbandry, the growth of which are inter-connected.
- Deputy Chief Minister Sushil Kumar Modi, who also holds Finance portfolio, while speaking at annual pre-budget meeting of finance ministers of all states and Union Territories said during last budget the Central government had announced Rs. 400 crore for increasing productivity in Eastern region as part of ushering the areas into second green revolution, I would request special programmes to be announced in the budget to start the rainbow revolution in the eastern region which would not only increase agricultural productivity but also the per capita income of the majority of people dependent on agriculture, farmer enhancing food security for the country.
- A study by International Food Policy Research Institute tracing constraints and opportunities for sustainable

agricultural production in Bihar says the state has abundant water, sun shine and labour but is facing certain problems which puts impediments in its agriculture growth. It identifies these constraints as small and fragmented land holdings, low productivity, underdeveloped institutions, poor infrastructure and low public investments.

- It came out with the facts that for rice, 47 per cent of the areas are still achieving a yield of less than 1.5 tonnes per hectare. For wheat, 36 per cent area is still achieving less than 2.0 tonnes per hectare, for maize about one third area is achieving an yield of less than 1.5 tonne a hectare and pulses 47 per cent of the areas is still getting an yield of less than 0.8 tonne per hectare.
- Among key *abiotic* constraints it came out with the finding, that 41.4 per cent of cropped area is flood-prone, about 2,199 thousand hectare (flood years 2004-05, 2007-08, 2008-09, 2010-11).
- Besides, the state is facing drought every year for the past 4-5 years. In 2012 also poor monsoon hit the state hard like other parts of the country, when majority of the districts witnessed deficient rainfall.
- Other constraints identified were soil acidity and water logging.
- As part of adequate institutions & poor infrastructure the study highlights that thinly spread markets which come to 0.6 per thousand square kilometre. The credit is only Rs 3,930 per hectare (March 2008 as per Annual Credit Plan), Insurance awareness still in infancy and cold storage still rare with only 1.5 per thousand square kilometre.
- As part of suggestions as how to *unlease* opportunities, it recommended 4-pronged strategy—innovation, institution, incentives and infrastructure.
- It suggested to harness untapped yield reservoir, *leverage* power of improved technologies, utilisation of fallow lands and promotion of agriculture diversification.
- It also highlighted the nud for creating special agricultural zone like one for cereals, fruits, vegetables, poultry and fish, attraction of corporate sector for investment in markets, agro processing and land development. For

strengthening institutions it recommended land reforms (consolidation, ownership), pro-poor (smallholder) agriculture, collective production and marketing, contract farming and farmer cooperatives. It also suggested strengthening credit-insurance services and extension services.

- Due to efficient handling of the situation, Bihar managed to minimise the adverse impact of poor monsoon in 2012. Contrary to the rest of the country, sowing of kharif crops had shown a marginal increase despite rainfall deficiency estimated at between 20 to 32 per cent in Bihar this year with 28 districts badly hit due to shortage of rains.
- Plantation of rice, sugarcane and coarse cereals in Bihar on August 8 had been recorded for more than the normal level of 2 lacs hectare for the period.
- According to the official figures presented in Parliament by the then Union Minister of State for Agriculture Harish Rawat, while the area under rice had increased by 0.8 lacs hectare in Bihar even in this adverse condition that of sugarcane and coarse cereals rose by 0.7 lacs hectare and 0.5 lacs hectare respectively.
- Mangala Rai, Agriculture Advisor to the CM, said that efficient and timely handling of the situation by the state government prevented severe damage to agriculture.
- To avert the crisis due to rainfall deficiency, the Bihar government took remedial measures like providing subsidised diesel and 5-8 hours of uninterrupted electricity to rural areas. About 80 per cent of the transformers were changed to maintain smooth supply of power in the summers, he said. The state government decided to provide diesel subsidy of Rs. 20 a litre to boost irrigation of kharif crops due to uneven distribution of rains in some districts.
- While the Union government woke up to the situation arising out of weak monsoon in August and announced 50 per cent subsidy on diesel for protecting stand in crops, Bihar had such taken steps much earlier.
- Along with agriculture, steps have been taken to strengthen storage of foodgrains and make public distribution system

more effective and corruption-free.

- According to official information, in order to enhance the food grains storage capacity 423 godowns are being constructed at the block level with a total capacity of 2.84 lacs metric tonne. Administrative sanction of Rs. 206.57 crore has been accorded for 423 godowns.
- Ration and Kerosene coupon scheme has been in place on the basis of which people living below poverty line can get food grain and K-oil at fixed rate and quantity.
- Vigilance committees have been constituted at panchayat level in rural areas and ward level in urban areas to keep an eye over functioning of PDS system. There is also a monitoring committee under Sub Divisional Officer (SDO) for checking irregularities in the distribution of subsidised food items to beneficiaries. Village gramin banks have been established in 13 flood-prone districts suffering from deficiency of foodgrain. These are—Muzaffarpur, Sitamarhi, Sheohar, East Champaran, West Champaran, Darbhanga, Madhubani, Samastipur, Saharsa, Supaul, Khagaria, Katihar and Bhagalpur). Different colours of cards are being provided to different categories of benficiaries that includes Red for BPL, yellow (Antydaya) and green (APL) have been made available to beneficiary families.
- A pilot project has been launched in Gaya district to track vehicles transporting food grains by using global positioning system (GPS). Sub-Divisional Officers holding Jan Adalat, once a month have been told to dispose complaints related to Targetted Public Distribution System (TPDS) system speedily.
- The state Food and Civil Supplies minister Shyam Rajak says there is a plan for effective monitoring of of the PDS system through laptops to check corruption. He says the scheme would start by year end. Accordingly the state government would appoint 535 computer assistants at block level to assist the block supply officials to feed the information of PDS. All the computer assistants would be given laptops for the job. The information on daily basis will be available with the head office of food and consumer protection department. There are 45,000 ration shops in

Bihar.

- The state government has been demanding cash transfer for its beneficiaries under TPDS system instead of providing grains but the Centre has not acceded to its demand. Bihar has also protested the Centre about number of beneficiaries under the subsidised food scheme. While the Centre is allotting foodgrain quota for the scheme for about 70 lacs families based on the report of Tendulkar Committee, the state government disputes the figure saying it is around 1.60 crore. The Bihar government has extended benefits to the left over families from its own resources till the Centre updates its figure of beneficiaries after a fresh survey.
- Significant steps have been taken for development of Animal Husbandry and fisheries, which promises rich dividends to the state's agro-based economy. In the Rs. 3,200 per hectare annual premium under Fisheries Insurance Scheme, the state government is bearing half the amount while the rest half is paid by the beneficiaries themselves as part of agreement with Oriental Insurance Company.
- Rs. 6.89 crore has been earmarked for backyard goat rearing scheme and backyard poultry rearing scheme for schedule castes.
- Silos have been established at nine places—Patna, Munger, Bhagalpur, Saharsa, Purnea, Muzaffarpur, Darbhanga, Chhapra and Banka for storage of liquid nitrogen for artificial insemination.
- Plan is afoot for establishement of 300 new primary veterinary hospitals in addition to the existing hospitals.
- To promote goat rearing, 30 per cent bank subsidy is provided to progressive goat farmers. Under the scheme to bring veterinary services to the doorsteps of cattle owners, 266 out of the 527 primary veterinary centres/ district veterinary centres, building construction has been completed. Free distribution of good breed goats in 10 districts has been undertaken with a view to improve goat breeds in the state. Chicken production and distribution started through the breeding of low input technology

poultry with the collaboration of Central Poultry Zone, Patna, Bhagalpur and Purnea regional poultry zones.

- Out of the 1,401 defunct artificial insemination centres in the state, 550 have been revived, bringing the total number of functional centres to 950.
- Fodder production has been started on available wastelands in the four government animal breeding farms of the state. This will serve as emergency fodder for cattle in times of natural calamities. Production and distribution of free fodder blocks in flood affected districts have been made through establishment of fodder banks.
- Animal Health Protection Programme has been initiated to protect cattle from infectious diseases and to deliver immunisation to cattle at the owner's doorsteps.
- Under Public Health Engineering work, full drinking water coverage has been provided to 11,277 rural habitations in 2011-12. Ground water discharge facility is provided to 1,340 elementary schools and built in 9,688 schools.
- Construction of toilets for 412,456 BPL families and 1,25,387 APL families have been done. Besides, 1,500 mini piped water supply scheme with solar pump completed in 26 drought-prone habitations, work of such 400 schemes are in progress. Work has started on mini pipe water supply schemes with solar pump in 270 water scarce remote rural habitations and on 165 such programmes with electric pumps. 1,737 hand pumps have been sunk under the scheme sanctioned for sinking of hand pumps on recommendations of local MLAs. Water quality testing of 44,122 hand pumps have been done.
- 29 cremation ghats have been modernised under Mukti Dham Scheme for development and modernisation of cremation ghats.
- In 39 arsenic affected habitations of Barhara block of Bhojpur district, multi village piped water supply scheme has been completed. In 200 habitations of Buxar, Vaishali and Patna districts such schemes are in progress. In fluoride affected habitations of Khaira in Munger district, work of multi village piped water supply scheme based on surface water is in progress.

- Installation of stand alone drinking water purification system in 3,831 schools under Jal Mani Scheme is in progress, in 3,331 school installations done.
- Water supply schemes for Bodhgaya, Khagaul, Phulwarisharif, Danapur and Muzaffarpur, sewerage and sewage treatment schemes for Begusarai, Buxar and Hajipur as well as drainage scheme for Rajgir being executed by Bihar Urban Infrastructure Development Corporation at a cost of Rs. 617.38 crore.
- Purnea, Katihar and Begusarai have been accorded the status of municipal corporation.

Power

- Electricity crisis is the bane of economic development of Bihar. Due to power shortage, process of industrialisation is not gaining momentum.
- Chairman of the Aditya Birla Group, Kumar Mangalam Birla had said during the global summit on Bihar held in Patna in February 2012 that heavy industry captains are hesitant to invest in the state without proper electricity supply. He advised Chief Minister Nitish Kumar to first create enough power supply for rapid industrialisation.
- Birla's remark is not an off the cuff remark. Bihar's power generation capacity is 80 MW from its two power units—Barauni Thermal power station and Muzaffarpur Thermal power station. The state which consumes around 700 to 850 MW daily, completely depends on supply from NTPC for power distribution.
- Only about 50 per cent of Bihar's 38,475 villages are electrified though it does not necessarily mean they receive power. The per capita annual electricity consumption in Bihar is about 75 KWH (Kilowatt per hour) as compared to all India average of 600 KWH and 895 KWH of Punjab. Even Gurgaon, a satellite town on the outskirts of the national capital, per capita electricity consumption is about 1,265 KWH.
- Long power cuts are a routine affair in the state capital whereas far off districts feel lucky to get a few hours of power particularly in summers. Many villages continue to live in darkness.

- Battling worst power crisis situation, the Chief Minister recently led an all party delegation to Prime Minister Manmohan Singh to seek 50 per cent of power generated at NTPC's two upcoming plants in the state. The team also sought coal linkages to expansion plans of 500 MW Barauni thermal power unit.
- In a memorandum submitted to the Prime Minster, the delegation requested for allotment of 50 per cent of electricity generated at Barh stage-II and Kahalgaon stage-II thermal power plants to the host state of Bihar as in the case of 14 NTPC units coming up in different states.
- "This is a minimum demand we have made to the Centre and we hope the Union government would fullfill it," the CM said.
- The Barauni power station is a central government unit hence it is the responsibility of the Centre to ensure regular coal supply for its two units of 250 MW each which are in the final stages, he said.
- Responding to the call of power-starved Bihar, the Centre has agreed to allocate 50 per cent of electricity from upcoming 1320 MW NTPC Barh unit in Patna district.
- In a letter written by the then Union Minister Sushil Kumar Shinde to Bihar Chief Minister Nitish Kumar, the Central minister also agreed to expeditiously take up the fuel linkage issue related to Barauni expansion with the Coal ministry.
- In his letter, Shinde said as immediate help DVC (Damodar Valley Corporation) will supply 100 MW of power to Bihar.
- Further, NTPC's Nabinagar stage-II will be expanded to 3x660 MW instead of 2x660 MW, he said adding, NTPC has been advised to tie-up the requisite inputs urgently in consultation with the Bihar government.
- On coal linkages for two upcoming units of 25 MW each at Barauni, Shinde said "Bihar may apply for coal block allocation for case-II projects at Lakhisarai, Pirpainti and Buxar etc. Ministry of Power will recommend for allocation of coal blocks to ministry of Coal.
- NTPC says that after completion of nine upcoming NTPC

projects in eastern states likely in the next five years, Bihar would receive another 2960 MW of electricity. The total installed capacity would be 14,890 MW out of which allocation for Bihar would be 2,960 MW.

- Acting on its promise, the Centre has announced 1,183 MW power from its two future NTPC plants at Barh.
- Thanking Centre, Bihar Chief Minister Nitish Kumar has written another letter to then Union Power minister Sushil Kumar Shinde seeking allotment of 15 per cent of the unallocated power from the two plants expected to start functioning by 2015-16.
- Asian Development Bank has agreed to extend a loan of Rs. 650 crore to the state for strengthening its electricity transmission and distribution system in seven cities to cut down power losses. The cities chosen for the purpose are Biharsharif, Bettiah, Motihari, Bhagalpur Ara, Buxar, Samastipur and Begusarai.
- Under the scheme, new quality transformers would be installed and transmission lines would be laid for uninterrupted electricity supply. The loan facilitated by Union Power Ministry would be operational till 2016.

SOCIAL JUSTICE WITH PARTICULAR REFERENCE TO MUSLIM WELFARE

- The new dispensation in Bihar embarked its journey six years ago on the plank of development with social justice. Working on the agenda the government launched several welfare measures for all social classes. Welfare of weaker sections including women, children, extremely backward castes, minority muslims, Scheduled Castes and other Backward Castes have been given preference to bring them into the mainstream of society.
- The result is that Chief Minister Nitish Kumar is getting support from all shades of society. Peoples say that the difference between the past and present is that an honest attempt has been made to ensure that the fruits of the welfare schemes reach the beneficiaries.
- Nitish Kumar government won accolades from across the country for pioneering decision of reserving 50 per cent of

the seats in panchayats and urban local bodies for women. Many other states have since then emulated the concept.

- With woman at the helm of affairs, panchayats have started delivering results.
- A visit to Harpur Rai gram panchayat in East Champaran district reflected the commendable work done there. Headed by mukhiya Bacchi Devi, who was honoured by then President Pratibha Patil in 2008 for making the panchayat free from open defecation by ensuring 100 per cent toilet arrangements. Every household has a toilet in the panchayat.
- Asked how the idea hit him, Bacchi Devi, who has the distinction to win panchayat head election from a general seat beating 9 male rivals, said during door-to-door election campaign, I found that many houses did not have a toilet, as a result women particularly faced great difficulties. The very first thing I did after winning the election in 2008 was to provide liberal loan under the welfare scheme for construction of toilet. Awareness campaign was also launched to make around 10,000 inhabitants of the panchayat spread in an area of 1300 acre understand its advantage. The financial assistance was only a one-time affair, now people themselves spend money for upkeep of the toilet in their homes, she said.
- The Panchayat is now venturing into newer fields of encouraging people to plant trees and also making arrangement to provide training to females in making wax lamps. An NGO has been roped in for the training programme at panchayat office. The result is encouraging, she said and added that if the wax lamps work grows at larger scale the panchayat would take the job of marketing them in Patna and other towns.
- In the face of shortage of power, the panchayat has also successfully experimented with solar lights installed on roads at important junctures. Bacchi Devi said while hoisting tricolour on the occasion of Republic Day this year that girls securing first division in matriculation will be given Rs. 5000 assistance and also a solar lamp that will help them study.

- Initially, the concept of reserving half of the panchayats for women witnessed problem of "mukhiyapati" (husband of mukhiya) ruling the panchayat by proxy. With the spread of awareness and government tightening of screws the malady has been removed.
- In the realm of women empowerment, to prevent exploitation of women, helpline for women and short stay homes at district level have been erected and strengthened. The government is providing uniforms to 30.7 lacs children enrolled in anganwadi centres at the rate of Rs. 250 per child. Social audit is being conducted in every anganwadi centres on 15th of each month (take home ration distribution day) as a check to prevent irregularities in the functioning and financial activities of these anganwadi kendras. To address the problem of children health and malnutrition, nutrition day is being organised and observed at all anganwadi centres in collaboration with the health department.
- To prevent female foeticide, registration of births and encouragment to female birth is given through "Mukhyamantri Kanya Suraksha Yojna".
- To provide financial assistance for marriage of the poor brides "Mukhyamantri Kanya Vivah Yojna" has been launched. To provide financial assistance for girl inmates of government run corrective and refuge homes, who have acquired age and whose parenthood and caste identities are unknown, "Mukhyamantri Sanwasin Kanya Vivah Anudan Yojna" is in place.
- The government chose to display the healthy tradition of planting a tree within the residential premises in village Dharhara in Bhagalpur district on the birth of a girl child as theme of its tableau on the occasion of Republic day function at Rajpath in 2012.
- In the child development sector, strict supervision is being made on running of ICDS programmes whose monitoring is done through SMS. Inspection and supervision report is sent through e-mail. Action is being taken with the coordination of health department and UNICEF to distribute Zinc tablets/ORS packets in 10 districts of the

state. State child protection unit and district child protection units have been constituted in all the 38 districts. Child Welfare Committees have been constructed for all districts.

- Special thrust is being given for welfare of OBC, EBC, SC and ST.
- For the identification and development of *mahadalits*, "Bihar *Mahadalit* Development Mission" has been constituted. Several schemes launched for welfare of mahadalits (weaker sections among dalits) including "Mukhyamantri Mahadalit Poshak Yojna", "Mahadalit Toilet Construction Scheme" and "Mukhyamantri Jeevan Dristi Yojna." 72,517 toilets have been constructed under the toilet scheme for *mahadalit* by the end of 2011.
- Capacity of SC/ST residential schools increased to 40 per class. This will increase the number of students in these residential schools to 28,320 from the current strength of 16,680. There has been a 25 per cent increase in allocation for better quality food and equipment (clothes, learning materials etc.) for students in class 5 to 12 in government SC/ST residential schools. Security guard training has been imparted to 4,130 mahadalit persons under the "Dasrath Manjhi Kaushal Vikas Yojna".
- The rate of scholarship for SC/ST students have been enhanced three-fold from April 1, 2011. Against a monthly scholarship of Rs. 15 to a child of class I to IV the amount has been raised to Rs. 50 for each student per month. Similarly for class V and VI the scholarship has been scaled up to Rs. 100 a month from Rs. 30/month earlier. For class VII and X it is Rs. 150 monthly vis-à-vis Rs. 55 earlier. For hostel purposes the revised amount is Rs. 250 per month for each of SC/ST student now from Rs. 80 a month earlier. Similarly, for sports scholarship (for coach and students) Rs. 700 per month for 6 months is sponsered now as compared to Rs. 200 per month in the past.
- Focused attention is being paid for the welfare of minority in the state who constitute a significant chunk of the state population (roughly 12 per cent).
- The biggest decision to win trust of minority muslims for

the government was to ensure speedy trial in infamous Bhagalpur communal riots of 1991 in which over 1000 innocent were butchered in the wake of demolition of Babri mosque at Ayodhya. Many persons accused in the riots including the main accused Kameshwar Yadav, have been put behind the bars after expeditious trial in a special court.

- After long persuasion to the Central government, the Nitish Raj finally won a compensation of Rs. 3 lacs for victim of Bhagalpur riots at part with those of anti-sikh riots in 1984.
- Efforts are made on to reclaim properties of victims of the riots which were snatched away from them by the local influential people.
- A unique result of all these efforts to wash tears from the eyes of muslims in Bhagalpur is that a BJP man Syed Shahnawaz Hussain is Lok Sabha member from there. This is his second term from Bhagalpur constituency which has sizeable muslim voters. The RJD which claims itself as champion of muslim failed to defeat Shahnawaz on the seat. Posters were painted on walls across the town, also known for its silk, displaying miseries of muslims during Gujarat riot and there leaders speeches were laced with reference of Narendra Modi and communal riots in the western state post-Godhra incident. There had been no report of any communal tension in Bhagalpur or elsewhere in Bihar during Nitish regime for the past over half-a-decade.
- Besides, ensuring communal harmony in the state, the government is running several welfare schemes for the minority muslim community. Minority welfare directorate has been constituted for welfare of the minority community. Two new schemes "Mukhyamantri Alpsankhyak Rojgar Rin Yojna" and "Mukhyamantri Alpsankhyak Siksha Rin Yojna" have been launched.
- Under Mukhyamantri Alpsankhyak Rojgar Yojna started from 2011-12 financial year, soft loan through State Minority Financial Corporation is provided to unemployed hailing from minority community for starting some work on their own. Under the programme for which a sum of

Rs. 1100 lacs was allocated in 2011-12 fiscal, young male and female belonging to minority community whose family income do not exceed Rs. one lacs yearly gets soft loan at a rate of 5 per cent per annum for self-employmet. A maximum sum of Rs. 5 lacs is given under the programme.

- Similarly, under Mukhyamantri Alpsankhayak Siksha Rin Yojna a sum of Rs. 4 crore was earmarked in 2011-12. Under the programme, soft loan is provided by Minority Financial Corporation to benficiaries for pursuing tehnical and higher education. The beneficiary of the scheme whose family should not exceed Rs. 4.5 lacs annually gets a loan of Rs. one lacs annually for a maximum period of five years is provided for pursuing medical/technical/ITI/BEd/ Law and Management courses.
- Work is in progress for equipping all the minority hostels with computer, internet and soundless generator. There is special arrangement for coaching for competitive examinations in these hostels.
- A sum of Rs. 10,000 is given to students belonging to minority community for securing first division in matriculation. The scheme was started by Bihar State School Examination Board (BSSEB) in the year 2007. A total of 2,627 students benefitted from the programme in the inaugural year itself, which went up to 5,688 and 12,969 in 2008 and 2009 respectively. In 2010 this soared to 20,225.
- Minority welfare department's budget has been increased manifold. Before 2005 (when RJD government was in power in the state since 1989) the annual budget of the department was Rs. 34 in 2004-05 which rose to Rs. 251.52 crore by February 2, 2012 in the fiscal 2011-12.
- The sincere efforts to reach to the minority muslim community is hugely appreciated by its citizens. The growing trust of the muslim community inj Chief Minister Nitish Kumar could be gauged from the fact that keeping him a sort of guaranter the minority people even voted for candidates of its NDA ally BJP the last Assembly election at many places.
- Nitish Kumar has also kept its ally under tight control;

the glowing example of which is not allowing Gujarat Chief Minister Narendra Modi infamous for 2002 communal riots in his state to campaign for BJP candidates neither in general elections nor assembly polls. During national executive meeting of BJP in 2011 to protest advertisement given in some newspapers regarding flood in Koshi by Modi supporter, Kumar had cancelled a scheduled dinner he had to host for the BJP leaders including L K Advani at that time.

- Due to growing faith and clout among the minorities particularly muslims, Nitish Kumar has managed to break the winning formula of "MY" (Muslim Yadav) of the previous RJD regime. The Lalu Prasad party which endeared itself among the muslims by stopping rath of L.K. Advani and getting the BJP stalwart arrested during his Somnath to Ayodhya rath yatra kept winning elections after elections for 15 years starting from 1989 on the basis of solid vote bank among muslims and his fellow castemen yadavs. The two together constituted around 35 per cent of the state population. Another advantage of this combination was MY was applicable in majority of the 243 assembly constituencies because of widespread presence of the two across the state.
- The MY first developed cracks in 2003 elections when Ramvilas Paswan's Lok Janshakti Party (LJP) in combination with Congress and Left parties dented the muslim vote bank of the RJD. Though Paswan's party did not win much of the seat particularly those of muslim dominated but it took away a sizeable vote of the minorities thus giving a blow to Lalu's party.
- During campaign , Paswan, who had fielded a large number of muslim candidates, raised serious questions about RJD's commitment towards their welfare.
- With the help of defectors from LJP, Nitish Kumar managed to cobble up numbers to form the government. But, the then Bihar Governor Buta Singh did not call him to form government. The Governor's decision was challenged in the Supreme Court which ultimately gave a

ruling against the Governor. Nitish Kumar took a Nyay Yatra across the state to mobilise support among people against this injustice. The campaign succeded and riding on popular sentiments against RJD, JD(U)-BJP won majority seats in 2005 assembly elections and Nitish Kumar became Chief Minister. Carrying hopes of common man, Nitish Kumar government won the trust of people and came with a thumping majority back to power in 2010 state assembly polls.

- Lalu Yadav's RJD which had fought elections with LJP got a severe drubbing. Same was the case of Congress which on behalf of its General Secretary Rahul Gandhi had decided to go alone to test poll waters. Congress number went down from 10 to 4 in the 2010 polls in the 238-member Bihar Assembly. The Bihar poll also raised questions over charisma of Rahul Gandhi who had rigorously campaigned in the state.
- The ruling JD (U) and BJP increased its tally by a substantive number. Riding on the popularity of Nitish Kumar, Janata Dal (United) won 117 seats alone followed by BJP whose number multiplied from 54 in the previous assembly to a huge 91. Minority muslim voters had played a vital role in decimating RJD and giving a landslide victory to Nitish Kumar. With Kumar standing as a guaranter, BJP which has never curried favour with muslim voters anywhere in the country, also got a large chunk of their votes which resulted in its tally growing substantially. Nitish Kumar is undoubtedly the most popular leader for muslims today in Bihar. Carrying forward the trust, Kumar is also not leaving stone unturned to address the issues of muslims and also work for the community welfare. Lalu Prasad's party received further losses as its many leaders particularly those belonging to muslim community deserted him for JD (U). Former Union Minister Mohammad Taslimuddin, Monazir Hasain and Lalu's trusted aide and former state minister Shakeel Ahmad Khan are among the prominent leaders in this category. Ramvilas Paswan's party also faced similar situation leaving the two (Lalu and Paswan) high and dry.

- Continuing with the bad luck, the RJD-LJP combine faced humiliation in the last General Elections, too. Lalu's party managed to win only four parliamentary seats including Chhapra won by Lalu himself (though he lost from another seat of Patliputra to his friend-turned-foe Ranjan Yadav). Paswan drew a blank, he himself losing from his traditional seat of Hajipur (reserved) from where he had created record in 1977 and had entered into Limca Book of record.

2

Micro Studies of Places of Eminence to Understand the Changes in Bihar

- Though development and relatively better law and order is prevailing across the state, the trend could be better understood through case study of a few important places. The writer visited these places himself and interacted with cross section of people to read the popular mind.
- Jiradei, birth place of First president of Independent India Dr Rajendra Prasad in Siwan district.
- Located around 10 km from district headquarters of Siwan, it is witnessing a marked change in life of people. In addition to be a place of eminence because of being associated with the first President, Jiradei is also home to former RJD strongman Mohammad Shahabuddin, whose native village Pratappur falls under Jiradei block.
- Apart from witnessing marked changes in roads, health and educational situation in the area, the biggest thing for them to cherish now is end of "fear factor" from mind.
- "Log nidar ho gaye hai (people have become brave), said Radha Krishna Prasad locally known as "TT Saheb" because he recently retired from the post of Railway.
- With the vegetables market in front of his house hubbing with activities, TT saheb said such things were not witnessed half-a-decade back when people feared venturing out of their homes after sun set.

- With police patrolling the area regularly, people have no reason to fear from anybody and a large number of them were seen buying vegetables from the fair late in the evening.
- Now people do not hesitate to return to their villages in the outskirts even late in the evening which no family could have thought of earlier, said Lal Babu Prasad, former District board member.
- "Now there is rule of law and nobody can dare to ride roughshod on people," said TT Saheb.
- Dr Rajendra Prasad memorial has been added with the facility of quality pitched road which earlier was in a dilapidated condition.
- "Despite being a place for pride, the memorial was witnessing utter neglect earlier...but thanks to chief minister Nitish Kumar everything has been set right now," said Shambhu Shrivastava, who lives near the memorial.
- Street lights have been repaired and the area is bathing in the flood lights.
- But, local citizens complained poor condition of government Ayurvedic hospital. Old timers say that Dr Rajendra Prasad used to get medicine from the same hospital even after shifting to Rashtrapati bhawan.
- Built in 1954, the Ayurvedic hospital is still flooded by people, Dr Aasher Shah, the doctor posted at the hospital, said.
- Quality of live is improved now as people could roam freely. Schools and hospitals are also functioning satisfactorily, Lal Babu Prasad, former district board member said.

Sitab Diara

- If the native place of Dr Rajendra Prasad is witnessing a quality change in civic facilities and lives of people, the natives of Sitab Diara, birth place of Loknayak Jaiprakash Narayan, are no less happy.
- Located on the banks of river Saryu in Saran district of Bihar and around 150 km from Patna, Sitab Diara has tasted electricity in 2011, 64 years after the Independence.

- Sitab Diara's tryst with power coincided with the rath yatra of BJP veteran L K Advani, which kicked off from here in October 2011.
- Power supply has been arranged from Jayprakash Nagar grid in Uttar Pradesh on the other side of the Saryu river, Bihar Minister and local BJP MLA Janardan Singh Sigriwal said. Payment for the electricity is made by Bihar State Electricity Board (BSEB), he said. The responsibility to maintain smooth supply of power rests with the Panchayat.
- According to the arrangement, the village with a population of about 18,000 is witnessing 8-12 hours of electricity in a week during daytime and almost for the same duration in the night in alternate week.
- "We are watching modernity now after so many years of Independence in which Loknayak played a prominent role," Binod Shrivastava, a local resident, said.
- Sigriwal said even before arrangement of electricity supply from Jayprakash Nagar, he had put solar lights at main junctures of the village from his own fund.
- Besides, electricity, Sitab Diara will soon have a 3-km metallic road from Gariba Tola to Lala Tola (where JP was born and which still has his thatched house). The road will be a great relief for us particularly in the monsoon when it was difficult to come out of homes in the rains, said Shrivastava.
- The two sides of the river (one side Jayprakash nagar lying in Uttar Pradesh and another side Sitab Diara in Bihar) presented a picture of contrast. The portion under UP had metallic road, electricity and other civic facilities while Sitab Diara was a nondescript village living in darkness, Binod Shrivastava, who is the local postman, said.
- "But, now with electricity and roads, we do not feel inferior to our neighbours on the other side of Saryu," he said.
- Shrivastava said another piece of comfort for the locals is that there is no more incident of theft of their cattle.
- "Thieves used to take away our cattle tied outside the house but now because of a vigilant police the theft has stopped," he said.

- Deputy Superintendent of Police, Saran, Vijay Kumar corraborated the fact. "No incident of cattle theft has been reported from Sitab Diara in the last one year...Sitab Diara is free of crime now," he said.
- Kamla Charan Verma, cousin of JP, who heads Jay Prabha Memorial trust (named after JP's wife) is a happy man.
- "With the village having access to electricity, roads and improved hospital and school, we are enjoying development now," says the octagenarian.
- Government Middle school at Lala Tola, where JP had his initial education is also wearing a new look. Rooms of the school where around 500 boys and girls study, have been repaired and whitewashed to give a pleasant look to the institution.
- The school had almost converted into a "khandhar" (ruin) where people were hesitant to send their wards. But, the place is now cynosure of everybody and no student wishes to miss the school now, said Sanchit Yadav.
- Sigriwal said a library, museum and other developmental institutions have been planned for Sitab Diara in the near future.
- In an obvious reference to Rashtriya Janata Dal President and local MP Lalu Prasad, Sigriwal said, "people gained politically by using JP's name but totally neglected development. We as the true disciple of Loknayak have tried to pay our homage to the great socialist leader by carrying development of the place, Sigriwal said and added that Chief Minister Nitish Kumar keeps a close watch over condition of Sitab Diara. Motihari, District Headquarters of East Champaran district, Motihari occupies an important position in history because it was from here that Mahatma Gandhi had launched satyagrah, his greatest weapon against British rule.
- Motihari is also the birth place of reputed writer James Orwell. Recently, it was in the news because of tug of war between Chief Minister Nitish Kumar and Union Human Resources Development Minister Kapil Sibal over location of a central university. While Kumar was insisting that the university should come at Motihari, the Centre was in

favour of Gaya citing its proximity to the state capital and better infrastructure.

- After days of discussion and relenting to constant pressure of the CM, the Centre at the end agreed to establish central university at both Motihari and Gaya with separate campuses. Bihar which had no central university earlier will have two now. Bowing to the Bihar government repeated representations, the Centre allocated two universities to Bihar, one each at Motihari and Bodh Gaya.
- Recently, the Union Cabinet cleared a proposal to bring an amendment to the Central Universities Act for enabling setting up of two central universities in Bihar. This is the second exception made by the Union government for setting up two central universities in a particular state, the first being Jammu and Kashmir. The decision to set up a central university at Motihari along with the one at Gaya put an end a prolonged slugfest between the Centre and the Bihar government over the issue. But, the Union Human Resources Development minisrty said there would be no additional allocation for Bihar and the Rs. 240 crore meant for the state would now be divided among the two universities.
- Recently, Nitish Kumar shot off another letter to Sibal demanding to name the University at Motihari after Mahatama Gandhi for whom Motihari, was the "*karambhoomi*" (work place).
- Despite of its mooring in the history, Motihari had turned into a horrible place six years back like many other towns of Bihar.
- Kidnapping, loot, murder and rangdari were rampant. The criminals were so daring, they could loot someone on the main road in the broad daylight and nobody could do anything about it, Sanjay Pandey, a local said.
- Hardened criminal used to take extortion money from shopkeepers from behind the bars and nobody had courage to say no to them, locals said.
- But things have changed for the good now.

- "People do not hesitate to return to places on the outskirts of the Motihari town even in the mid-night," Pandey said.
- Former state cabinet minister Braj Kishore Singh, said, "this is the golden period for Champaran."
- Earlier, due to bad condition of roads a journey to historic places like Kesaria and Areraj associated with the great Samrat Ashok, which are around 50 km from the district headquarters, used to take almost 3 hours but with good quality of roads the journey has been reduced to less than an hour, Sanjay Pandey said. Kesaria and Areraj where Ashoka pillars have been found, are visited by a large number of foreigners particularly from China and Japan.
- Braj Kishore Singh, who is heading Gandhi memorial in Motihari is happy that due to improvement in road leading to the memorial, people of visit has increased manifold. "Earlier on best of the days not more than 100 people used to visit the memorial but now the footfalls has increased to 300-400 per day," he said.
- Tarkeshwar Prasad said hospitals and schools are wearing a new look now.
- The house of Millenium writer James Orwell is another important address for tourists and locals of Motihari. The Nitish Kumar government has recently provided Rs. 32 lacss for construction of four huge sized gates leading to Orwell house and upkeep of Orwell known for his literary pieces like "Animal Farm" and "Nineteen Eighty Four".
- Orwell was born in this house in 1903 and he died in 1950.
- Talking about sadar hospital Motihari, Tarkeshwar Prasad said earlier people used to visit the hospital only after death for post-mortem. But, now things have changed and people first prefer to come to the sadar hospital in case of ailment instead of making long que outside the house of some doctor, he added.
- With change in environment, every institution is working at its own level.
- The classic case is of Harpur Rai panchayat. The mukhiya of the panchayat had gathered nirmal gram prize from President Pratibha Devi Singh Patil for making people

understand the advantage of a toilet at their home, said head of the Panchayat.

- Mukhiya of the panchayat Bachhi Devi said with the help of fellow villagers the panchayat has planted trees alongside the roads for greening the village. The panchayat comprising of four revenue villages and 10,000 odd people is well connected with a four-km metallic road from the main road.
- In view of interrupted supply of electricity, the panchayat has got around 35 solar lights installed at main junctures.
- Bachhi Devi said in her speech on Republic Day this year she announced that the panchayat will give Rs. 5000 to a girl student securing first division in matriculation examination. Along with cash the meritorious student will also get a solar lamp which will help him/her to do studies even if there is no power, she said.
- The panchayat with the help of an NGO is running a special training session of wax lamp making for girls and women to add up to their income. They assemble in groups in the panchayat bhawan for special classes in making of wax lamps.
- "When the work progresses later on panchayat will think of making arrangaments for organised marketing of the wax lamps in Patna and other towns of Bihar," Bachhi Devi said. The mukhiya adds that they are thinking of new ideas to make lives of people of the panchayat happy only because the environment has changed and there is no fear of criminals and rowdy elements.
- The administration is also promoting the traditional profession of making shirt buttons out of shells which was popularised by Mahatama Gandhi during his stay here in course of agitation against forceful plantation of indigo.
- Braj Kishore Singh said he was surprised when during one of his visit to Germany he went to market to look out for button of his shirt and the shopkeeper showed him the button made of shells from Champaran. Nalanda district with its headquarters at Biharsharif, which is also the home district of Chief Minister Nitish Kumar, is cynosure of all eyes. Situated at around 70 km from the state capital,

Nalanda district has witnessed an allround development.

- "Nalanda can be easily said to be the model district of resurgent Bihar," JD (U) Chief Whip and MLA from the district Shrawan Kumar said.
- Improved roads, hospitals and schools have brought qualitative changes in the lives of people here.
- "The 45 km strech from Daniyama to Biharsharif with potholed roads was a painful ride for us. It used to take at least 3 hours to cover this much distance," said taxi driver Sikandar.
- But, now with high quality roads and trees planted alongside the road, the journey time has been reduced to 45 minutes to one hour, he said.
- Primary health centre at Noorsarai wore a new look, so did the Middle school at Godhpar in the district.
- Improvement in infrastructure has added up numbers of tourists to Rajgir.
- "With improved roads and regular police patrolling people roam around in Rajgir till late in the evening which was not possible before," Pawan Kumar, a book seller at the station road said.
- He himself was kidnapped from near hot water *'kund'* (fall) in 2003 and taken away after being bundled in a sack. I remained in the clutches of criminals for 17 days before police rescued me from them, he added. But, now there is no incident of kidnapping or criminals intimidating anybody, he said pointing towards policemen on patrol duty in the main market place.
- With a new Engineering college and Sainik school, Nalanda is witnessing golden time after a long.
- Chief Minister Nitish Kumar early this year opened a women police station, first of its kind in Bihar, at Biharsharif. The police station is completely manned by women officers and where cases related to women will be lodged only. There is a proposal to open such all-women police station in all 38 districts of the state in phases.

- Darweshpura in Ekangalsarai block of the district is hogging the limelight for recording highest productivity of potato and rice in the world.
- A farmer, nameshake of chief minister Nitish Kumar, has managed to raise 729 quintal of potatoes applying organic farming techniques. The previous record was registered in the name of Netherland for producing 45 tonne per hectare.
- Earlier, a group of farmers in the same village had created a world record for producing 224 quintal of paddy per hectare using the system of rice intensification (SRI) method.
- Union Agriculture minister Sharad Pawar had referred about this rare achievement of farmers of Darbespura in Parliament during budget session of 2012.
- Buoyed by these success, Chief Minister Nitish Kumar has expressed confidence that the dream of a second green revolution could be attained in a short span of time.

Darbhanga

- The prominent town of Mithilanchal, Darbhanga is also witnessing an improved quality of life now. Swanky mall in the heart of the town around 110 km from the state capital and high rise buildings are sufficient to show the trend of modernity that has touched the town.
- "A two bed room flat is booked for a relatively high price of Rs. 8-10 lacs at the very time of foundation laying of the apartment in Darbhanga, said Mukesh Kumar Jha, who runs an NGO in the district.
- Rent of a two bed house has soared to Rs. 4,000 per month from a paltry sum of Rs. 800-1000 a month earlier, he said highlighting the change in quality of life in the town. Almost all known car companies be it Hero Honda, TVS or other brands have their showroom in Darbhanga. Similarly, all prominent private banks including HDFC, ICICI and Axis banks have their branch in the town.
- The things are rosy not only in the town, but has touched interior areas, too.

- Construction of Rashyari bridge over Kamla river has brought a sort of revolution in the lives of people of Kirathpur block of Darbhanga, bordering Saharsa. Natives of Rashyari, Bawur and Khaisa Jamalpur in the block are happy that they could reach their villages in lesser amount of time due to metallic road constructed.
- "Earlier, residents of Khaisa Jamalpur, the last village of Darbhanga on the border of Saharsa, used to give a boat as gift in the marriage as people had to sail in the boat to reach the village after road ended at Ghansayampur," said Mukesh Kumar Jha, the state coordinator of Dr Prabhat Das Foundation, an NGO working for the upliftment of people.
- But, after construction of 15 pillared Rashyari bridge in 2011 these villages could be reached by motorable roads in less amount of time. A journey from Darbhanga to Kamsul which is around 55 km earlier used to take nearly three hours due to rugged roads but now it could be covered in less than an hour, Jha, who also brings out a newspaper in the name of the foundation, said narrating his personal experience. Remote areas like Tengha and Jai Jai pandit village in Tardi block could also be reached through motorable roads, something people had thought not possible within their life time.
- Benipur sub-division, about 25 km from the district headquarter, which had no hospital earlier has now a 100-bed referral hospital which is thronged by a large number of people. Likewise every village has a middle or primary school. Roughly 73 High schools have been added with the plus two facility in the district.
- With high standard of cleanness and availability of free medicines, Darbhanga Medical College and Hospital (DMCH) is witnessing rush of people from the district and also neighbouring areas.

Patna

- State capital Patna has become lively with addition of many facilities and improved roads and flyovers.
- A new Mall cum PVR complex P & M opened by film maker Prakash Jha in Patliputra area has become

favourite of families. Many other food joints and restaurants have added to mobility of people. Families and elderly could be seen enjoying evening in new Budha Smriti Park which has come up at the site previously housing jail. The park was inaugurated by Tibetan spiritual leader the Dalai Lama on the invitation of Chief Minister Nitish Kumar.

- Construction of nearly a dozen flyovers in the city has reduced traffic congestion where the vehicles used to move at a snail pace earlier. Broadening and maintenance works of Bailey Road has added up the speed of vehicles.
- With improved law and order situation and added infrastructure, Patna is witnessing a boom in real estate. The price of a flat in Patna is no less than that prevailing in Delhi or Noida. Apartments have come up in every nook and corner of the city.
- Many parks and roundabouts which were lying unused because of their ill keep have been converted into lively destinations by handing them out to private parties who maintain them.
- Sanjay Gandhi Children Park in the heart of the town which had been used as dumping ground for garbage and which used to be preferred destination of pigs now, is a lovely park with pleasant grass and scores of swings and other playing facilities. Children with their mother make a beeline to the park every evening.
- The big chunk of land near old secretariat which was a mound of garbage has been transformed into a beautiful park.
- Development is not confined to the city area only but has travelled to interiors also.
- Actor-politician Shatrughan Sinha, who is Lok Sabha member from Patna Saheb, said he has got roads constructed in Fatuha, Patna Saheb and other far off areas.
- The state government has decided to implement an ambitious "Green Patna" intervention. Under this 30,000 trees would be planted in the next three years. This intervention follows the fairly successful programme of development of a large number of parks in Patna, which

was elicited a positive response from the general people.

- Bhagirathi Vihar, a Ganga river restaurant run by Bihar State Tourism Development Corporation (BSTDC) was recently inaugurated by the Chief Minister. This restaurant would not ony provide a multi cuisine fare to Patna foodies but would also afford a good view of the Ganga river. The restaurant has been constructed at Gandhi ghat at a cost of Rs. 97 lacs by BSTDC.
- This two-storied restaurant comes close at heels to the successful floating restaurant namely M V Ganga Vihar launched recently by the corporation. Built in the shape of a huge boat, this restaurant would offer mughlai, chinese, south Indian and continental food.
- The Tourism Development Corporation has also made arrangements for organising Ganga arti twice a week on every Saturday and Sunday on the line of one done at Varanasi. The corporation is also contemplating some packages based on Ganga river and river sports to lure more tourists to the state.
- Like some of these district towns other towns and cities are also witnessing positive changes in terms of roads, hospitals and other civic amenities.

3

Reflections of Bihar Growth

Reflections of Bihar's Growth Story

- The resurgence of Bihar is not for nothing. The impact of transformation of the state on the path of development is all encompassing. One of the most important reflections of the change is the stup drop in migration of labourers from the state. Cycle manufacturers and big farmers of Punjab have been crying shortage of workers mostly from Bihar which is effecting their trade. Recently, the Punjab government demanded special fund for farm mechanism to overcome the problem of unskilled labour shortage in the fields.
- Train loads of Bihari workers alighting at Jallandhar or Ludhiana is no more a common sight. There have been reports of owners dangling lofty incentives to these labourers including free mobile sets and bicycles to lure them return to work.
- Reports of labour shortage is also pouring in from other places like Surat or Himachal Pradesh where also despite being a hilly state Bihari labourers were overwhelmingly engaged in construction work in interiors of Kangra and Chamba districts.
- Resurgence of the state has brought about a welcome change in attitude of people towards Biharis who used to be looked down upon earlier. The word Bihari is no longer considered insulting now. People from the state who used to hide their identity earlier to escape abuses in Delhi,

Punjab or elsewhere from locals, now move proudly. Biharis are no more a subject of lampoon, but the masters of the crowns.

- The centenary celebration of Bihar recently in Delhi and Mumbai attracted tremendous response. In the broad map of India noble Bihar shone like a sun!
- A survey report recently brought to light the fact that migration of unskilled labourers from Bihar in search of livelihood to places like Punjab and Delhi has declined by over 26 per cent; thanks to large scale development works ordered by the Nitish Kumar government in the past six years. The central government flagship MGNREGA scheme is also contributing to this by providing job near home.
- "Flight of unskilled workers from Bihar to different parts of the country came down by 26.53 per cent in 2006-08 as compared to 2001-03," the survey carried by non-governmental body "Bihar Institute of Economic Studies" said.
- The survey work was carried out in the districts of Siwan, Madhubani, Saharsa, Bhagalpur, Nalanda and Rohtas to assess the impact of government initiatives to curb migration ratio, the Institute Director Pyare Lal said.
- The study found that the maximum migration was to Punjab (26.36 per cent) followed by Delhi (21.34 per cent), Maharashtra (15.06 per cent), Haryana (11.72 per cent) and West Bengal (5.86 per cent).
- It found that lack of employme]nt opportunity was the single most important reason (54.17 per cent) for outward movement of labourers.
- A survey by the state Labour department estimates drop in workers migration from Bihar by 30 per cent. It attributed this to large-scale development works being carried out in infrastructure sector like roads, bridges and hospitals and also strengthening of the education system.
- Labour Minister (state) Janardan Singh Sigriwal said the department has ordered for a fresh labour survey. Preliminary reports emanating from the survey done extensively in districts like Saharsa, Kishanganj, Purnea

and Araria which witnessed mass exodus of people to Punjab, Gujarat and Delhi have indicated a further decline from the earlier estimates of 30 per cent in migration of blue colar workers from Bihar in search of livelihood.

- The final report of the survey being carried out jointly by officials of labour department and those from A.N. Sinha Institute of Social Studies and NGOs is expected soon.
- Former head of market regulator SEBI C.B. Bhave had recentlly, while speaking at an international seminar at London, said that Bihar under Chief Minister Nitish Kumar is doing "very well", but the state's development has led to labour shortages hurting the country's construction industry adversely.
- Due to many new job opportunities and improved conditions in Bihar, not many in the state now migrate to other states in search of livelihood, Bhave said. This is adversely effecting the construction industry particularly, Bhave said at a high profile seminar of top business and financial leaders from India and London.
- "The construction industry is suffering serious labour shortage. For years, the industry depended on labourers from Bihar, but now when they take leave and go home, 70 per cent do not return to work on construction projects in different states," he said at the seminar organised by the City of London.
- Nasser Munjee, Chairman of the Development Credit Bank, also noted the improved conditions in Bihar, particularly in cities, and added that much needed are to be done for development to reach rural areas of the state.
- Noted agricultural scientist Mangla Rai, who is currently Chief Minister's advisor on agriculture, said with highest growth rate of 14 per cent in 2010-11, Bihar is now giving a run for their money to developed states like Gujarat and Maharashtra.
- Apex developers body CREDAI Vice-President Getamber Anand said, "It is true that lesser number of labourers from Bihar are arriving now. We have to arrange local hands. This has pushed up the wages for construction jobs in Delhi and NCR."

- Labour Minister (state) Janardan Singh Sigriwal said the target is to bring down the migration of unskilled labourers to zero.
- BJP spokesman Rajiv Pratap Singh Rudy said, "The NDA government is creating job opportunities at home itself so that people don't have to move out in search of livelihood."
- The pang of labour shortage is particularly felt in Punjab where cheap labourers from Bihar was an important component of booming agriculture and manufacturing sectors. People have thought of different motivational items to tempt labourers return to work after a visit to their home towns on the occasion of festivals.
- News reports say that facing acute labour shortage mainly due to less influx of migrant labourers particularly from Bihar, employers in Punjab are doling out freebies like mobile phones and bicycle to lure them.
- Witnessing almost 30 per cent labour shortage, nearly 5,000 small and big manufacturers of bicycles and parts in Ludhiana popularly known as "bicycles capital" are facing threat of closure, traders said.
- Some of the leading names in the bicycle manufacturing in Ludhiana including Hero, Avon and Rolex are also grappling with the problem of labour shortage.
- "The workers are also given mobile recharge coupons of Rs. 50 to Rs. 200 denominations to talk to their families as an incentive to dissuade them from going home," D.S. Chawla, former President of United Cycle and Parts Manufacturing Association said.
- A bicycle costing around Rs. 2,500 is given either free or for a paltry sum to these labourers so that they can paddle to their work place, P.D. Sharma, president of Chamber of Commerce and Industries (Punjab) said.
- The scenario is still more stark in the farm sector. Facing acute shortage of hands particularly during sowing and harvesting seasons of wheat and paddy, farm owners have almost doubled the daily wages of labourers to Rs. 300 as a special incentive, farmer Inderjit Singh said.

- Chawla said earlier migrants while going home used to request their employers to keep their jobs intact till they return, but today the situation is just opposite.
- Now many employers make a call to homes of labourers and even deposit additional money in their bank accounts to motivate them to travel back to work, Chawla said.
- Que of lorries and tractors outside Railway stations to ferry migrant labourers used to be a common sight in the past, Chawla said adding they are not to be seen now.
- Chawla said bicycle manufacturers had in the recent past met Prime Minister Manmohan Singh, former Finance Minister Pranab Mukherjee and Industries and Commerce minister Anand Sharma to press for a special fund for technology upgradation to help survive in the backdrop of restricted supply of labour force.
- Reports of labourers coming for menial jobs like in construction to Himachal Pradesh also suggest a drop. Mohammad Taufique hailing from Siwan said that earlier Bihari labourers and masons were involved on a large scale in construction of houses and other building not only in Shimla but also in interiors like Kangra, Chamba and Sirmaur. But, now with work available at home itself, these labourers are not enthuasiastic to come so far to earn livelihood, Taufique said.
- Drop in migration and reports of progress back home have brought about a welcome change in peoples, perception about Biharis outside the state. Earlier, people from Bihar were a subject of ridicule in other states. People used to hide their identity to escape such humiliation. Bihari dialect had become language of comedy in many a Bollywood movies which put them in a poor light.
- But, the situation has changed drastically now and Biharis are no longer looked down upon. Though there has been reports of a section of locals instigated by fledgling political party MNS and also by Shiv Sena are targetting people from Bihar and Eastern Uttar Pradesh in Maharashtra as part of their popular version of politics, but on the whole

there has been an image changeover for Biharis everywhere.

- BJP leader Shatrughan Sinha says not only within the country but in other countries like USA, UK, Germany and France, NRIs enquire about the state. Many persons from abroad participated in the Bihar Global summit meet at Patna in February 2012.
- Chief Minister Nitish Kumar, whom many people think as a potential candidate for Prime Ministership in near future, commands respect outside the state, too. Notwithstanding political rivalry many central ministers and Congress Chief Ministers have praised him for bringing Bihar back on the path.
- The centenary celebration of Bihar on completion of 100 years of formation of Bihar evoked tremendous response in Delhi and Mumbai.
- At a function held at Burari ground New Delhi, a large number of people mostly hailing from Bihar converged to take part in the function to celebrate the glory of completion of 100 years of coming into being of Bihar when it was carved out of Bengal by the Britishers on March 22, 2011.
- Addressing the function, Chief Minister Nitish Kumar said people from the state forms around 20 lacs of the total population of the national capital.
- He said with such a huge presence, Biharis could bring Delhi to a grinding halt if they decide not to work for one day. In the same breadth he said despite constituting a large chunk of population, Biharis are not a "burden" on Delhi's economy but in truth adds up to its growth. He narrated the growth story back home and asked migrants to keep doing good works for betterment of other places also. Twenty people from the state were honoured on the occasion for excelling in their fields of activities.
- Those honoured included former Foreign Secretary Shyam Saran, Cricketer Syed Saba Karim, singer-actor Manoj Tiwari and noted doctor A.K. Singh.

- Though similar function at Mumbai was mired in controversy following some outlandish comments made by Maharashtra Navnirman Sena chief Raj Thackeray and also Shiv Sena leaders over Nitish Kumar's strong reaction against targetting of Biharis in Mumbai and other parts of Maharashtra and his credited statement that nobody requires a visa to travel to Maharashtra.
- During his speech in Mumbai Nitish Kumar highlighted positive contribution of Biharis in economy of Maharashtra, he exclaimed the rich culture and tradition of Maharashtra.
- Though his political rivals like Lalu Prasad and Lok Janshakti party leader Ramvilas Paswan read this as "surrender" by Nitish Kumar before MNS and Shiv Sena, but people from Bihar residing there thronged the venue in a large number reflecting growing enthuasiasm among masses to associate themselves with changes taking place at their glorious home Bihar. Moreover, a leader has a severe voice, an d severe mind.

4

Sound Bites on Bihar Growth

- The resurgence of Bihar has been appreciated within home and out of country as well. The Bihar's growth story has attracted positive sound bites from Tibetan spiritual leader the Hon'ble Dalai Lama as well from many visiting foreign ministers and trade representatives. Microsoft giant Bill Gates and Japanese Prime Minister have recognised the changing face of Bihar and showed interest in participating in the process.
- Within the country, many union ministers have acknowledged the transformation of the state, a prominent member of the BIMARU states, is undergoing. Though political compulsions stop them from making public statement but, in private conversation many of them voice support and wonder why did not it happen earlier.
- "In the last few years, Bihar has shown good progress in the economic sphere," said Montek Singh Ahluwalia, Vice Chairman of Planning Commission.
- Acknowledging good performance of Bihar, a prominent member of BIMARU states, the Planning Commission has increased the annual budget size of Bihar for the year 2012-13 to Rs. 28,000 crore from Rs. 24,000 crore in 2011-12 and promised all help to ensure sustainable growth of the state.
- Delhi Chief Minister Sheila Dixit had said to CNN-IBN, at Indian of the Year function that we "Have to learn the technique of good governance from Nitish Ji."

- "The biggest reason for Bihar's development is restoration of the rule of law. Other states should learn from Bihar," said Swaminathan S Anklesaria Aiyer, eminent economist and journalist.
- The state drew kudos from outside the country, too.
- "I am very happy to be in Bihar. The work of Nitish Kumar is quite encouraging," said Tibetan spiritual leader His Excellency Dalai Lama.
- The Nobel laureate, who visited Patna in 2010 to inaugurate the Budha Smriti Park that has come on the same venue where existed the previous district jail, spoke encouraging things about the state. Recalling his Patna visit, the Dalai Lama said Nitish Kumar attributed his success in Bihar to Lord Buddha. To this I said Lord Buddha had been path-shower to the world particularly and his strong message went to the world from Bihar.
- The Dalai Lama, who has been living in India since 1959, has also on a number of occasions referred to Nalanda University, the seat of learning for the world in ancient times.
- In August 2012, an 18-member parliamentary delegation from Pakistan led by Senate leader Jahangir Badar visited Bihar and met Chief Minister Nitish Kumar.
- Badar said he and his fellow visitors were glad to get an opportunity to visit Bihar and lauded the prevailing atmosphere of peace and tranquility and communal harmony in the state.
- Bihar has registered tremendous growth in the past decade which was a matter of research, Badar said and congratulated Nitish Kumar for ushering in development in the state through exemplary leadership.
- Badar said members of Pakistani Parliamentary delegation will tell their countrymen about the growth story of Bihar and would like them to emulate the hard work of the people of Bihar for their prosperity.
- He extended an invitation to Nitish Kumar to visit Pakistan and share his experience with the people and leaders of the neighbouring country so that they could draw inspiration from him.

- Another Senator Haji Md. Adeel extended invitation to Nitish Kumar on behalf of Punjab Chief Minister Mohammad Shahwaj Sharif, brother of former Pakistan Prime Minister Nawaz Sharif and said his visit and interaction with the Pakistani leaders will enable them to adopt measures taken by him to eradicate corruption.
- Nitish thanked the Pakistani delegation for sparing time to visit Bihar and promised to make a trip to the neighbouring country by year end. According to media reports during his interaction with the delegation, Nitish Kumar told them about prevalence of lawlessness and mushrooming of *kidnapping industry* in the state prior to his taking the rein in 2005, making an obvious reference to RJD regime, and how his government worked hard to establish a rule of law in the state and ushered it in an atmosphere of peace and tranquility.
- Lalu Prasad, who had made a trip to Pakistan with a team of Indian parliamentarians earlier had made people of that country crazy with his earthly jokes and jest. The then Pakistani President Parvez Musharraf had also acknowledged Lalu's popularity and his rustic humours.
- But, Nitish praise of Pakistan is far more sincere and for the concrete works he led to pull the state out of the mire. Nitish led a delegation from Bihar to Pakistan for a week in Nov. 2012 and received a leader for achievements of his goveernment. Pakisitan President Asif Zardari dinner for him and delegation.

  During visit to Pakistan people showed eagermen to know about "Bihar Model of evelopment".
- But, Lok Janshakti Party leader Ramvilas Paswan, who is working with Lalu Prasad for ouster of Nitish Kumar regime, did not like him telling the Pakistani delegation about bad situation prevailing in Bihar during his predecessor's time.
- "Kumar has shown immaturity by discussing internal political issues and vilifying the performance of his predecessor in Bihar," he was dejected.
- "It goes against political ethics when you run down your adversary before foreigners. I never raised domestic

political issues whenever I met representatives from foreign countries as "we are duty-bound to put up united face and represent the country during interaction with a foreign country and visitors from there."

- The LJP supremo said he, too, has visited a number of countries, including Pakistan but never discussed domestic political issues with them.
- Microsoft Chief Bill Gates said, "This is not the Bihar of old. Now schemes and roads are visible. Immunisation against dangerous diseases has shown positive.
- The changed scenario in Bihar is encouraging foreign countries to go for greater engagement with the eastern state which in the past was never a favoured destination for them due to bad law and order with poor redress, and not so good governance.
- The US Under Secretary of State for Political Affairs, Ambassador Wendy R Rehman recently went to Patna to meet Chief Minister Nitish Kumar and Governor Devanand Konwar before attending a meeting to discuss trends in development and governance throughout the state.
- Sherman was accompanied by US Embassy Charge d'Affairs A Peter Burleigh.
- She attended a meeting of some of Bihar's leading entrepreuners, think tank analysts, community leaders, NGO activists and state government officials to discuss trends in development and governance throughout the state and potential challenges faced by them.
- "Bihar is on the move...Bihar has emerged as an inspiring model of positive change and good governance. Bihari society in general and its youth in particular appear eager to create new opportunities for economic growth and development," Sherman said.
- Expressing interest in the growth story of Bihar, the United Kingdom has also shown eagerness to explore opportunities for British companies to invest in the eastern state.
- The keenness was expressed by UK Finance Minister George Osborne, who had called upon Chief Minister Nitish Kumar in Delhi by early April 2012.

- Osborne was accompanied by James Bevan, British High Commissioner to India, JO Johnson, MP and Paul Rennie, Political Head, British High Commission.
- "UK Finance minister wanted to explore the investment opportunities available to British companies for participation in the growth story of Bihar," a statement quoting the British Finance Minister said.
- The chief minister informed them that huge investment opportunities are available, particularly in power sector, professional education (engineering, management, law and skill development) and agro-based industries.
- The noble CM told them that his government had given highest priority to good governance which included enforcement of rule of law, transparency in functioning of the government, investment in infrastructure, strengthening delivery of public services like health and education.
- He invited the British Finance Minister to the state to which Osborne assured he would like to know more about Bihar and would come to the state during the next visit to India.
- Encouraging response emerged from Japanese Prime Minister Yoshihiko Noda also to whom Chief Minister Nitish Kumar had met in the national capital early 2012.
- The Japanese Premier appreciated that under Nitish Kumr leadership Bihar has made significant progress. "Now Bihar has maximum potential for development," Noda was quoted saying.
- He also noted that a number of Japanese tourists visit Bihar specially Bodhgaya, an important place for Budhists. He pledged support for Nalanda University not only for physical infrastructure but also for intellectual bilateral exchanges, and requested the wiser CM to identify specific area for collaboration.
- The Bihar CM informed him about 10 year roadmap for agriculture development and requested for cooperation in terms of Japanese technical and financial assistance for food processing and logistics for improving storage capacity

and road connectivity so that farm produce can reach market quickly and farmers get their judicious due.

- The CM informed this will help in bringing second green revolution in eastern India and Japan can play a significant role. He also appreciated the Japanese PM support for Nalanda University and the improving infrastructure for Buddhist tourist circuit. The CM also informed that state government is building a world class museum and has taken the services of renowned Japanese architect for this.
- Israel Ambassador to India Alon Ushpiz, who paid a visit to Bihar in August 2012 end said, his country would step up cooperation with Bihar in the sectors of agriculture, solar energy, water harnessing and health insurance.
- Cooperation would be increased in agriculture sector with thrust on promotion of horticulture, dairy, fishery, besides green vegetables and water area, Ushpiz said after meeting Nitish Kumar.
- "We will have two centres of excellence in agriculture sector," he said. The cooperation in the energy sector with the support of the union government would also be extended particularly in the field of solar energy.
- He praised the works of Nitish Kumar. Describing Kumar as impressive, competent and effective leader of Bihar where, he said, tremendous development works and economic growth was taking place.
- In 2010, Prime Minister of Bhutan, Lyonchen Zigme Y Thinley visited Bihar. During the beginning of 2011, Home Minister of Bhutan, Lyonpo Minjur Dorji also visited Bihar. On the invitation of Bhutanes PM, Nitish Kumar visited Bhutan from May 4-7, 2011.
- In course of his meeting, the Bhutanese Prime Minister expressed his deep appreciation of the improved facility being provided by the Bihar government to Buddhist pilgrims in Bodh Gaya and Rajgir.
- The Bihar CM said if the new hydro power projects being constructed in Bhutan with India's help, are commissioned in time, the state government would be requesting for its

due share of energy in these projects from the Government of India. The Bhutanese Prime Minister pointed out that by 2020, an additional 10,000 MW of installed capacity would be created in Bhutan.

- In his meeting with Home Minister Lyonpo Minjur Dorji, the CM stressed on the need for a mutual understanding between Bihar State Tourism Development Corporation and Bhutanese Tourism Council to provide necessary facilities to Bhutanese pilgrims. The Home Minister of Bhutan readily agreed to this idea and said a package consisting of transportation, boarding and lodging facilities to Bhutanese can be offered by the Bihar State Tourism Development Corporation.
- The Bhutanese Home Minister also expressed the desire of the Royal government to construct a stupa in Budha Smriti Park, Patna. The CM agreed to the proposal.
- The transformation in Bihar has positive impact on neighbouring Nepal with which the state shares a long international boundary.
- A prominent weekly newspaper of that country *Nepal Times* edited by renowned Nepali journalist Kunda Dixit took a cover story on Bihar.
- He wrote an article in this newspaper in 2000 bemoaned the fact that the Nepal bordered India's poorest state and asked: Is Nepal going the Bihar way?
- Bihar used to be a *pejorative* word, a *collective noun* that encapsulated everything that was wrong with India—inequality, injustice, insurgency and indigence. It was synonymous with crime, corruption and caste.
- Nepal was in the same boat, but somewhere deep inside we felt superior because we thought there was a place worse off than us. This was proven by number of beggars on Thamel sidewalks, scavangers on our dumpsites, the barbers from Darbhanga, vegetable vendors from Motihari and plumbers from Muzaffarpur, the newspaper wrote.
- How the tables have turned?
- Bihar is being rapidly transformed after the election of reformer Nitish kumar in 2005, the newspaper noted.

- One indication of this is that the barbers, traders and plumbers have gone back to Bihar, not just from Kathmandu but from other parts of Nepal, too.
- After hitting bottom, Bihar had nowhere to go but up. For the past several years the state has posted an annual 11 per cent growth rate even though its mineral rich South wasbeavated out from its symmetrical wholeness.
- Bihar is an example of how elections can throw up enlightened and accountable rulers, the Nepal newspaper observed.
- For all those who despair about Nepal ever turning around, we can only say if Bihar can do it so can we. Our leaders should stop promising that they will turn this country into Switzerland or Singapore. Is Nepal becoming another Bihar? let's hope so, the newspaper said.
- Bihar attracted lavish praise from tiny country Seora Leone. Deputy Chief Minister Sushil Kumar Modi, who paid a visit to the African country early in 2012 to attend a conference on growth and development in the capital Free town drew rich praise from that country.
- Addressing the audience, Modi drew similarity between recent past of Bihar and Seora Leone despite being separated by distance and geographical differences. Like Bihar which suffered hugely for nearly 15 years starting since 1989 (when RJD ascended to power), Seora Leone was ravaged by the internal strife. Both the economies wish to come out of the period of darkness and usher into an era of progress, growth and peace.
- The Bihar Deputy Chief Minister told the audience about some revolutionary steps his government had taken like recruitment of retired army personnel in police force, speedy trial for keeping a control over law and order, Special Court Act to check corruption cases, Chief Minister, Ministers and officials making their assets public, seva yatra undertaken by the CM to know the results of development projects initiated for them and people's court hosted by the CM to give an opportunity to common man to vent their problems to him directly.

- During his stay there he met its President Ernest Bai Koroma, Vice-President Samuel Sam Sumana and other high dignatories and conveyed best wishes from people of Bihar to them. The Seora Leone leaders talked richly about resurgence of Bihar and showed eagerness to adopt the "Bihar model" of development in their roadmap of growth for their own country.
- Similarly, Singapore's External Affairs Minister Masagos Zulkifli who visited Patna early 2012 and met Deputy Chief Minister Sushil Kumar Modi voiced good words about development taking place in the state. The Singapore minister extended his country's help to Bihar in the field of water management and urban development. He also expressed eagerness to contribute in development of Nalanda International study centre.
- Zulkifli said his country is facing shortage of drinking water and has to purchase at least one-third of the country's requirement of water from Malaysia, rest they arrange from conservation of rain waters or by recycling the used water resources.
- The minister said Singapore has expertise in water management and urban development which it would like to share with Bihar. During talks with Deputy Chief Minister the Singapore minister was impressed with the measures taken by the state government to tighten law and order, improve roads and health arrangements.
- Mohammad Abbas, a Pakistani national who is now settled in the USA and living in Dallas, showered rich praise on Nitish Kumar for development of Bihar. "Lalu Yadav is very popular among immigrant Indians and Pakistani in Dallas. He merely played comedy and neglected development of Bihar. But, the present Chief Minister Nitish Kumar is properly utilising the limited state resources to usher the state on the path of development," Abbas said.
- Trinidad and Tobago Prime Minister Kamla Prasad Bissessar, who recently visited Buxar district of Bihar tracing her roots, credited the "soil of Bhelupur (in Buxar) for all her success and achievments."

- "Whatever I am today is because of the genetic make-up and DNA from the place of Bihar. I am the Prime Minister of my country because of blessings of this soil and this land of our ancestors," an emotionally surcharged Bissessar told a mammoth fraternity.
- Wearing *sari*, Kamla, 60, seemed to face no language bar as she made a forceful speech in English starting with *Bhaiyon and Bahno, Pranam*.
- She emphasised on the importance of her visit to Bhelupur. "If you don't know where you come from, you will never know where you are going to. I come from a great land of great people. I will urge all my countrymen to find out their roots."
- Kamla's great grandfather Ram Lakhan Mishra from Bhelupur village had set out for the Caribbean islands in 1889 as *girmitia* labourers. He had boarded Volga ship from Calcutta harbour on October 21, 1889.
- President of Mauritius Rajkeshwar Purryag shedded a happy tear as he returned to his family's Bihar village.

  Accompanied by wife Anitah Purryag the Mauritius President visited Wajitpur village in Masaurih sub-division of Patna disitrict from where his ancestors had migrated to Mauritius about 150 years ago.

  Tears rolled down from Purryag eyes on emotional reunion with people of his ancestors village. He thanked Chief Minister Nitish Kumar for making the trip possible by collecting the details of his root and providing him information about the place and its old citizen.

5

Life and Style of Nitish Kumar

- The son of an unsuccessful Congressman Late Shri Kaviraj Ramlakhan Singh who earned his living as an ayurvedic *vaid*, Nitish Kumar was born in village Kalyanbigha under Bakhtiyarpur sub-division in Patna district on March 1, 1951. His nickname is Munna.
- Nitish Kumar ordered among Ramlakan's five siblings– the first being daughters Usha, Prabha and followed by sons Satish and Kumar. The youngest is Indu.
- Kumar was a quiet person who from the beginning preferred privacy for himself.
- As a child Nitish studied at Sir Ganesh High School at Bakhtiyarpur co-founded by his father who was the school Secretary. Nitish showed no interest in sports. He did play traditional games such as marbles or *gulli-danda*, according to his friends.
- As a student he was good at mathematics from the primary level. His father wanted to see him in medical profession, but watching his obsession with math he decided to let him go for engineering.
- Nitish was also fortunate to have a good Hindi teacher Shambhu Sharma who ignited in him a reading passion for short fictions by Premchand, Ramvriksha Benipuri and Phanishwar Nath Renu.
- He was unfortunate to learn English in the school. Sir Ganesh High School used to have a headmaster keen to

teach spoken English to students. He would ask students keen to learn English, speak to him in that language while walking from school back home after the end of school. In his middle school level, Nitish and other students would envy those students speaking *phataphat angrezi* (fluent English). But, by the time he reached high school level, the teacher retired. The new English teacher confined himself to textbook and showed no special interest in encouraging student to speak English.

- As a student, Nitish Kumar, as his friend, recollect, was good. His good academic performance helped him win National Merit scholarship of Rs. 150 a month which made him rich among friends who would herd around him for merry-making.
- They recounts, Nitish was not a movie buff but loved to watch films of Raj Kapoor during his high school days.
- One of his friends, who was his classmate at Bihar Engineering College in electrical engineering in 1968, recounts that Nitish, he himself and two other members of their coram of four were not interested in studying engineering which they thought was imposed on them by their parents. He says, given a choice, Nitish would have loved to study Physics or Chemistry as he used to tell friends. Sometimes they would question wisdom of their parents' decision of enforcing engineering on them saying, engineers are corrupt hence the parents want them to join the stream.
- After graduating in 1973, Nitish travelled with his friends to Bokaro to register himself with the steel city employment exchange. But, within a couple of months, Nitish received a letter from Bihar State Electricity Board to join as a trainee and recruited as Assistant Engineer. Nitish travelled to Ranchi and joined but never worked for a day after that, as he did not want to get stuck in a job. The passion for politics kept him away from such fixed commitment.
- Before he could get final degree in engineering, he got married to Smt Manju Sinha on 22 February, 1973. She was daughter of Krishna Nandan Sinha, a well off farmer

and headmaster of the secondary school in his native village Sheodah in Hernaut.

- His friends recall that even after his father accepted the marriage proposal, Nitish wouldn't have the courage to go and see his would be wife at the Magadh Mahila college of Patna University where she was pursuing her graduation in sociology. He hesitated to go to the G.D. Women's Hostel, where Smt. Sinha stayed, despite the fact that his younger sister Indu was also an inmate there.
- His friends would always chide him for this. That one day, three of his buddies on rickshaw roamed around the hostel for hours. Finally, they succeded in having a glimpse of her. On return they told Nitish about their adventure. On this he said laughingly that now I have a certificate about her from three musketeers what else I want.

But, the marriage ceremony was not a smooth affair. His friends recount that it was traditional Hindu wedding and his father had agreed to take a cash of Rs. 22,000 from her father. Nitish had taken a silent vow not to accept any dowry and was totally against elaborate rituals of vedic marriage which was against Lohiaite commitment to a crusade against brahamanism. He insisted on marriage according to Arya Samaj which advocated simplicity.

- He insisted that he would do nothing except exchange garlands at the marriage ceremony and was against any ritual or festivity. The parents of the two families had no choice but to succumb to his wishes. Accordingly the function took place at Lala Lajpat Rai Memorial Hall in the heart of Patna. A large number of socialist leaders and workers had turned up. There were speeches attacking the cancer of dowry and opium of ritualism and applauding the revolutionary marriage. They hailed Nitish for this.
- In order to spread the message far and wide, the famous socialist journalist Jugnu Shardeya published an interview on the marriage with Nitish in the popular Hindi weekly *Dharmayug*.
- Nitish Kumar has a son named Nishi who studied in BIT Mesra. Like father, he is also a quiet personality and keeps away from media glare.

- Nitish Kumar's political career has not been smooth but passed through long phases of struggle.
- Nitish began his political career in 1969 as a member of the Socialist Youth Council, a front of Ram Manohar Lohia's SSP(Samyukta Socialist Party). Later he worked as a student leader in the Patna Science College. It was the Bihar movement of 1974, under Chhatra Sangrash Samiti, leading to the JP movement during the emergency, that catapulted Nitish to the state level.
- Like other fellow socialist leaders including Lalu Prasad and Bihar Deputy Chief Minister Sushil kumar Modi, Nitish Kumar's political career started under the tutelage of Lok Nayak Jaiprakash Narayan during his anti-emergency movement against the Prime Minister Indira Gandhi.
- He was detained in 1974 under the Maintenance of Internal Security Act (MISA) and also during emergency in 1975.
- He was first elected to Lok Sabha in 1989 by defeating veteran state congress leader Ram Lakhan Singh Yadav known as "Sher-e-Bihar" from Barh constituency .He was President of Yuva Lok Dal, Bihar from 1987 to 1989. He was made Minister of State for Agriculture under Chaudhary Devi Lal in the V.P. Singh government in 1990.
- He served as Union Minister, Railways and later in Surface Transport Ministry in 1998-99. In 1999, he resigned from Railways owning to moral responsibility following an accident killing 200 people at Gaisal in North-eastern part of India.
- In 2000, he was made the chief minister of Bihar but he had to resign after seven days pending a no confidence motion by the opposition. Later that year he joined as Union Agriculture Minister in the Atal Bihari Vajpayee government.
- From 2001 to 2004, he served as Railway Minister in the National Democratic Alliance (NDA) Cabinet of Atal Bihari Vajpayee. He was instrumental in creation of a East Central Railway (ECR) Zone out of Eastern Railway Zone overcoming strong resistance from Mamata Banerjee, who

was then part of NDA. The zone has its headquarters at Hajipur.

- In November 2005, Nitish Kumar led the NDA to a victory in Bihar assembly elections ending 15-year rule of Rashtriya Janata Dal of Lalu Prasad. Riding on his good performance, the JD(U)-BJP coalition was re-insteted to power with a thumping majority in November 2010.
- Political circles were agog with speculations, if Nitish had some bigger plans when the Janata Dal (United), the party with Nitish Kumar and Sharad Yadav as national president, break ranks with the BJP-led NDA over candidature of former Finance minister Pranab Mukherjee for presidentship and over his views in an interview to an English daily insisting on a "secular" PM candidate from NDA in 2014 which was seen as his disapproval of candidature of Gujarat Chief Minister Narendra Modi, who is talked about in some political circles as likely BJP nominee to take on Congress General Secretary Rahul Gandhi in 2014 parliamentary polls.
- The remarkable performances of Nitish Kumar in taking Bihar out of morass, pitchforking it on the path of development and establishing his unquestionable support among minority sections have triggered debates on him as among probables for Prime Ministership.
- Nitish Kumar has always tried to stay clear of this saying, his concern is development of Bihar and he is not preparing himself for the post. With the debate gaining more fodder, one of JD(U) minister in Bihar, Bhim Singh out of excitement asked the BJP to make Nitish the NDA PM candidate for 2014 general elections. He had cited a survey report in Bihar in which 62 per cent of respondents wanted to see Nitish on the PM post. The minister in context had been an associate of Lalu Prasad for a long time.
- Nitish did not liked it and reprimanded the minister for this following which Bhim Singh ate his words.
- "I regret my remarks in deference of the sentiments of the Chief Minister who expressed displeasure for airing my personal views in public," stated Rural Development minister Bhim Singh to a press.

- "I had expressed my views out of excitement and I regret that I should not have made such comments even in my individual capacity," he said.
- Nitish defended, pulling up the minister for shooting his mouth unnecessarily. "Bhim Singh's statement might have been taken as my endeavour to make a case for myself as NDA's Prime Ministerial candidate which is not the case," the CM said adding he had ruled himself out of the race and had consistently said the post should go to the largest constituents of an alliance at the Centre.
- Bihar Deputy Chief Minister and the BJP's most prominent face in the coalition government Sushil Kumar Modi also jumped on the debate. Modi had described Nitish as "prime ministerial material" and said he would play an important role in the 2014 elections.
- Thanking Modi for the praise, Nitish said he has already clarified his views on the issue.
- Though Nitish refuses to accept that he is a probable for the PM post he has made it clear to his senior partner BJP in the NDA coalition that Gujarat Chief Minister Narendra Modi should not be a nominee of the coalition for the post. He had made this clear to the then BJP national president Nitin Gadkari when he had come to attend the oath ceremony of Pranab Mukherjee as the President of the country.
- In view of small size of MPs of JD(U) does not convince of his chance to the post, but considering his widely accepted image among all sections of people, in the event of a 'hung' House, he might get a chance. Political pundits say if H.D. Deve Gowda and I.K. Gujral can become PM, why not Nitish who in any case has much wider acceptability among people even outside Bihar?
- Some encouraging remarks about Nitish Kumar from Congress during the time triggered speculations if he was warming up with the Congress for 2014 general elections.
- Though truth of all these would be known only when the time comes, one thing is very clear that Nitish's political birth has been in the mooring of anti-Congressism.

- His friend in his book has revealed that Nitish entered politics with a "wound" inflicted to his father, a freedom fighter and a prominent Congress leader in Bhaktiyarpur, who was wronged by his party by denying him nominations in 1952 and 1957 assembly elections from Bhaktiyarpur. Moreover, his baptism in politics has been done in the ideology of great socialist leader Ram Manohar Lohia who is considered a die hard critic of Congress.
- Nitish father had participated in freedom struggle at his home place. As a student of Government Ayurvedic College in Patna he was active in protesting visit of Sir Simon to Patna in 1928.
- Continuing to take part in Congress activities he was under police detention long thereafter as a result of which he was expelled from the college. He fought his case in court which decided his expulsion was unjust. He was re-admitted into the college though he lost more than a year.
- He was a marked man in the Patna district administration records due to his allegience with Congress.
- At Mahatma Gandhi's "Quit India" call in 1942 asking the British raj to pack their bags and go back, his fathersuspended his medical practice and plunged into the popular uprising. He was arrested, accused with heinous charges and sent to jail.
- But, his hard work was not suitably rewarded by Congress after Independence. The congress was dominated by two factions of upper castes—*Bhumihar* and *Kayastha*.
- He was dropped from the list for the 1951-52 elections because neither of the two Congress poll war rooms in Patna favoured him. As part of the deal struck between the two factions Tarkeshwari Sinha was preferred for Congress ticket for the Patna East (later Barh, which Nitish Kumar won five times) Lok Sabha seat and Sundari Devi (sister of late Prime Minister Lal Bahadur Shastri) for the Bhaktiyarpur vidhan sabha seat.
- He was sinurely hurt yet, after being persuaded by faction leaders that he would be given a seat at the next elections.,

he remained in the party and worked tirelessly to ensure victory of Sundari Devi.

- But the promise could not be kept. The two factions decided to renominate the same due from their respective previous constituencies which left him high and dry. He decided to teach Congress a lesson.
- He was joined by other local Congressmen including Acharya Jagdish, who, too, had aspired for a party nomination but was not entertained.
- They left the Congress and joined Janata Party led by the *raja* of Ramgarh. Acharya Jagdish became Janata Party candidate in Bhaktiyarpur, Keshav Prasad in Fatuha reserved seat and Ramlakhan in Barh in 1957 vidhan sabha polls. Though they could not manage to win the elections, Sundari Devi lost in Bhaktiyarpur. Keshav Prasad won at Fatuha.
- In contrast to his father, Nitish grew up as a die hard socialist. It was during his high school years that he began to be slowly attracted towards the socialist leader Ram Manohar Lohia's ideas on social equality —positive discrimination to backward classes, women untouchables and tribes and on primacy of mother tounge to Hindi over english in education and administration.
- The starting point of his attraction was repulsion towards Congress whose ministers both at centre and in the state were widely seen as self-seekers and caring little for masses. Nitish, who knew about it from newspapers and hearsay, sometimes argued with his father how he could go on supporting a political party that had degenerated from an organisation of selfless individuals to an association of selfish manipulators.
- His father much like other Congressmen, friends and acquaintences would regularly gathered at his place, responded with criticism of Lohia's irreverent "indecent" statements about phoney socialism of Jawaharlal Nahru. This would make Nitish more aggressive in the defence of his political icon (Lohia).

- Politically, it was coexistence of two ideological streams under one roof, but the father never forced his son to toe the line he himself had.
- Though he and his *bade bhai* (elder brother Lalu Prasad) are in two different parties and politically opposed to each other, they formed a formidable combination as leaders of backward castes in Patna University during the time of their student politics. When Lalu won the Patna University Student Union (PUSU) in 1973, an event that proved to be a turning point in the political career of Lalu Prasad, Nitish was responsible for mobilising votes in his favour from Engineering College. The two worked in tandem in several agitational programmes during 1974 JP movement and went to jail.
- Nitish had an important role in making Lalu Prasad the Chief Minister of Bihar for the first time in 1989. But, thereafter they could not walk together for long and Nitish parted with Lalu in 1994 to join Janata Dal and later Samata Party.
- Nitish electoral journey has been full of bumps. He succeded in winning his first state assembly election from native Harnaut constituency in 1985 after two failures in the hands of Arun Kumar Singh, a fellow Kurmi, who could successfully whip the caste sentiments of Kurmis by supporting the killing of Belchhi in which 17 dalits were killed, to teach them a lesson. He (Singh) himself was an accused in the killing which had led the Prime Minister Indira Gandhi to visit Belchhi in 1977.
- His friend recounts that seeing his son's deep interest in politics, his father without telling anybody travelled from Bhaktiyarpur to Patna to meet JP who knew him distantly from Independence days. After talking about Congress which went away from ideals promised after Independence, he told JP about Nitish and sought his blessings for him. It was not known how much it worked for him as JP was known for judging people on the basis of merit.
- During 1974 movement, JP had given a call to the students to keep away from classroom, for a year that would signify a rejection of the education system and also give an

opportunity to students to actively participate in the nation building.

- The call had initial success, but soon it descended in the minds of students as they feared they might loose a year. JP was worried that if students in Patna University returns to classrooms it would have adverse impact in other parts of the state, too, and the movement would lose steam. Most of the leading members of Chhatra Sangharash Samiti were in jails.
- It was in this circumstances that Nitish went from college to college addressing students. After hard persuasion, hundreds of students came out in his support and followed him to the office of Vice Chancellor. The VC, order to the students to go back to classrooms triggered a heated discussion with Nitish. The successful motivation of students for a boycott helped Nitish win appreciation of JP. It was after this day, JP started referring him by name and paying attention to his suggestions.
- Through sustained efforts thereafter Nitish came to be recognised as one of the two important student leaders in the Janata Party circles that came into being in 1980. Lalu Prasad was the another one. The thoughts gained currency that the two should be given ticket to contest Parliamentary election in 1980. Lalu who had been released from jail got nomination from Chhapra. Nitish missed the bus from Barh constituency as his release got delayed due to prison officials took longer to proceed his papers.
- But, chance came not much later as assembly elections was announced in 1985.
- His friends talked about him about his chance which he respondedors hundreds of factors work in election. But, he said he has promised his wife as it was his last chance and if he failed he would retire from electoral politics for evere. His wife was bowled by his vow to renounce politics and wanted him win to continue with his passion. She collected all her savings from profession as a school teacher and gave him Rs. 20,000; though not a royal sum but a huge moral booster for him.

- His regular interaction with people of Harnaut was a positive factor. During his campaign he told people that this was his last chance that he was seeking vote from them. Luck also helped him as Superintendent of Police of Nalanda district was Ram Chhabila Singh, who was relative of one of Nitish close friend Narendra Singh. This helped foil the use of muscle power of his rival Arun Kumar Singh, a hero of Belchhi massacre and who had defeated him in 1980 polls. The SP had asked his subordinates to keep an eye over sensitive booths. Nitish ultimately came out victorious with 50,000 votes, the beginning of good fortune for him.
- Though this was start of a good inning for Nitish, the big time came for him when he humbled tallest backward leader and a prominent Congressman Ramlakhan Singh Yadav in the Lok Sabha elections from Barh in 1989. Ramlakhan Singh Yadav was popularly called 'Sher-e-Bihar' and his defeat in the hands of Nitish suggested backward caste had transferred their support from Congress to Janata Dal.
- Lalu Prasad also won elections from Chhapra. At the national level, Nitish was seen among three or four top leaders of the Janata Dal. He had earned recognition from the Prime Minister V.P. Singh who made him Minister of State for Agriculture under Chaudhary Devi Lal qualified at his work for peasants.
- There was no looking back for Nitish thereafter. Nitish had been a popular figure in the politics even if he lost election to his friend and RJD candidate Vijay Krishna in 2004 from the same Barh constituency. But, he had won with comfortable margin from Nalanda seat, considered to be his pocket borough given the fact that his Kurmi castemen are in majority there.
- Nitish had played an important role in making Lalu Prasad as Chief Minister of Bihar by mobilising MLAs in favour of him in the triangular contest among Prasad, belonging to Devi Lal camp, Ram Sundar Das backed by V.P. Singh and Raghunath Jha propped up by Chandrasekhar whose gameplan was to win the vote of 12 Rajput MLAs which

proved costly for Das and he lost the race to Lalu Prasad. It is said that during this period many MLAs asked Nitish why he is mobilising votes for Lalu and is not contesting the post himself.

- The partnership between Lalu and Nitish continued and they together put pressure on the then Prime Minister V.P. Singh to implement recommendations of Mandal Commission report advocating 27 per cent reservations for Other Backward Castes (OBC) in the government jobs.
- But, as days passed and Lalu gained more control over state's politics due to unflinching support of his fellow yadav caste and muslims, which together constituted a winning 'MY' formula on the basis of their vast numerical presence totalling around 30 per cent of the electorates. Moreover, the MY combination had presence across the state and was not confined in a few pockets. This made Lalu Prasad an undisputed leader who would go around the town and boast, he was politically invincible and would rule the state for no less than 20 years.
- The RJD boss cleverly nourished this and paid pay attention towards MY and gave a damn to others. During one of the parliamentary polls he smartly played caste card by visiting a yadav dominated area of Chakaram and gave a slip to neighbouring areas of Sri Krishna nagar, Past and Telegrph colony and others where majority of the voters are from forward castes. Lalu's visit boosted confidence of his yadav castemen who would go around in the area claiming that he belonged to them and has nothing to do with others. This psychological boost raised the collar of his yadav castemen while others cursed him for giving a slip, the mental made divide on the surface among people helped Lalu consolidating his castemen votes.
- Lalu's growing arrogance and his utterances against forward castes created rift within the society and there were instances where people fought on caste lines. Forward caste people particularly those hailing from Bhumihar had a harrowing times. His in famous slogan of *Bhurabal saf karo* thereby meaning to finish Bhumihar, Rajput, Brahmin and Lala (Kayastha), the four upper castes, generated tension within the society.

- While, Bihar was burning in caste conflict, Lalu wound not mind as it further consolidated his position among backward particularly yadavas carrying it to local levels across the state. The surname yadav was revered by people out of fear that it might be connected to somebody sitting at higher position in the establishment.
- Besides, his two brothers-in-law—Sadhu Yadav and Subhas Yadav– one yadav or other gained notriety in every part of Bihar. While Surendra Yadav was dreaded in Gaya, Rajesh Ranjan alias Pappu Yadav held the sway in Kosi belt where he had a running battle with another strongman Anand Mohan Singh. Kaushal Yadav was a big name in Nawada, Kailu Yadav in Munger and Nawal Kishore Yadav, Babban Yadav and Anil Yadav were well known names in the state capital.
- There were events where somebody would intimidate common citizens by disguising himself as these popular names dreaded by the people. Once a resident of Boring road in the heart of Patna got a call in the name of one of them demanding handsome cash as extortion but after sustained inquiry by his relatives one among whom was a senior police officer in Uttar Pradesh, it was found that it was a traunt played by a local goon. But, the citizen lived in utter tension for more than a fortnight and he had stopped going to his office and family lived in shadow of fear.
- One of my friend told me an interesting story that he and his friends won handsome cash from a forward caste candidate in parliamentary polls in 2000. The very presence of a yadav among the group fetched rich cash from the candidate who thought the yadav would mobilise support for him among his castemen. He got more than one lacs rupees for the purpose though the nominee who was a national level leader now bite the dust. Later, Former PM I.K. Gujral contested that Lok Sabha election from Patna as a candidate of Lalu Prasad party.
- Yadavs who monopolise milk vending business in Patna exploited the situation and expanded their *gosalas* (cowsheds) in the vacant land where ever they found it

belonging to government or any individual. Nobody patronised them but the very surname yadav gave them a license and policemen would also not dare question them for encroachment. Even posh colonies in the state capital like Patliputra, Srikrishna Puri, Sri Krishna Nagar and Rajendra Nagar were not spared of such illegal occupations of vast tract of land.

- The matter became serious following which the Patna High Court gave a strong ruling stopping the illegal encroachments from government land mostly by these milkmen.
- Decimation of opposition in polls one after another during the period made Lalu Prasad an undisputed leader in Bihar while others looked pygmies in front of him. The party he belonged to became synonymous with his name. Nitish and others had not much say in the party affairs as Lalu took all the decisions himself.
- When water started flowing over head, Nitish considered as 'Chanakya' in the political circle of Lalu Prasad had no choice but to part company with his *bade bhai* (Lalu Prasad) in April 1994.
- The flash point came when 'Kurmi Chetna rally' was held at Gandhi maidan in February 1994 in which Nitish was a star speaker. The kurmis, who are a powerful backward caste like yadavs, had found immediate provocation in the absence of their caste from the list of backward classes released by the Central government for Mandal reservation and Lalu Prasad government in the state leaving them in the panchayat elections.
- Nitish and 12 other Janata Dal (George) who supported him decided to breakaway and wrote to Speaker Shivraj Patil. Sudha Shrivastava, a minister in Lalu Prasad government in the state also decided to say goodbye to him.
- On 21 April, 1994, they formed a new party Janata Dal (George) with George Fernandes as national president. Some other key personality in the Janata Dal including Bashist Narayan Singh, a minister in Lalu government ,

joined the rebel group. He is President JD(U), Bihar, currently.

- They formally launched Samata Party in October 1994 at a rally, dissolving Janata Dal (George) again, with George Fernandes as its President.
- Nitish with Fernandes and others began touring the state to highlight the ills of Lalu rule. Nitish had emerged as a rallying point of anti-Lalu campaign. Realising that Samata Party alone could not do much they decided to join hands with another major national party BJP before 2000 assembly elections and formed an important constituent of NDA.
- NDA made a huge gain landslide, winning 122 seats but fell short of the magic number of 163. Lalu was reduced to 124 seats from 167 five years ago. With no consensus candidate for the post of Chief Minister in BJP, choice veered around Ramvilas Paswan and Nitish Kumar. With strong backing from senior BJP leaders Nitish triumphed over Paswan and was elected as leader of NDA legislature (Bihar).
- Ignoring claim of biggest pre-poll alliance of RJD (with Congress and others) the Governor Vinod Chandra Pande called Nitish to form government ignoring claims of Rabri Devi (RJD). He gave seven days to Nitish to prove his majority on the floor of the Assembly House. But, as time came nearer, the numbers could not be mustered since Congress whose many leaders particularly those hailing from forward castes did not rebel, and muscle politician like Mohammad Shahabuddin working for Lalu. Nitish quit without facing the trust vote. This paved way for another rule of RJD under Rabri Devi. His time finally came when he led NDA to the marked point of majority in 2005 and furled on the hopes of common man. He became CM.
- Kumar is a widely travelled man. He has been to Singapore, Thailand, Havana (Cuba) and Moscow as a member of Indian delegation to the World Youth Festival in 1978; Australia and France as a member of Indian Parliamentary Delegation to the IPU Conference; France,

UK, Switzerland as the Railway minister. He attended Japan as an Agriculture minister to attend regional conference of UN's Food and Agricultural Organisation (FAO) in Yokohama.

- Always seen calm and composed, Kumar takes decision after meticulous study of a situation. He has brought about a sharp change in style of politics Bihar. He has been from the beginning a man having no-nonsence attitude.
- Due to his intelligent decision without making a political fuss, Lalu Prasad, whom he helped in becoming Chief Minister of Bihar in 1989, used to say, "Nitish seems to have teeth in his stomach." Lalu Prasad is elder to him by three years.
- Politician, and Bureaucrats, who were subjected to rustic just and humiliation of Lalu Prasad are adjudged back their rightful respect and dignity.
- Unlike Prasad who is known for his comic style and funny dialogues, Kumar has always been a no-nonsense man. A vegetarian, Kumar has been a workohlic spending almost 18-20 hours a day meeting people and experts for development of Bihar.
- When compared to the RJD boss, he sometimes appears not that an interesting personality but people close to him disagree. He shares light moments with friends but is always serious while on an official job. He went to see Prakash Jha's film "Apaharan" riding a rickshaw to Ashoka Cinema hall in Patna. Whenever he gets time he will go to some restaurant to have his favourite dish *Masala Dosa*. In season he likes to eat *hara chana* (green gram).
- A strict disciplinarian, Kumar would give no special treatment to his family. There was a time when even distant relatives of Lalu-Rabri received VIP treatment, people hardly knows kins of Kumar. People could not believe when a photograph appeared in a Hindi daily showing his *Behnoi* (sister's husband) standing in a serpentine que to buiy a form to apply for recruitment of teachers at primary and secondary level.
- An official, attached with the CM, once said. During a journey to a function, Nitish felt thirsty and asked for

water. The official out of courtesy reached to water bottle in the car and offered him but he refused to accept it saying he should concentrate on the work assigned to him. Later his personal assistant who was also travelling with him gave him water.

- Nitish's love for discipline and punctuality has brought about a major change in government offices as officials could be seen rushing to the office to be on his seat on time. Local trains are packed with employees in the morning who would make himself inside the train anyhow to reach office in the outskirts of districts on time. These trains are sometimes called *karamchari specials* due to unprecedented rush of government officials from to and fro to office in Biharsharif, Bhakhtiyarpur, Fatuha and other places everywhere.
- Unlike in past, 1 Anne Marg, the official residence of the Chief Minister is not abuzz with much personal activities. Majority of rooms in the bunglow is occupied by officials.
- A stickler to the time, Kumar would not entertain even his party MLAs if they come calling to him unscheduled. A statesman, even some people in the ruling NDA in famous as musclemen powers have learnt to live in discipline in his regime.
- The horse stables in 1 Anne Marg and cow sheds for a large number of cattles which used to occupy a large portion of the CM residence have been raged. The animals shelters have given way to creation of shed for people coming to meet the CM at *Janata Darbar*. People are offered chairs under the shed where the CM personally meets all of them unmindful of time, listen to their problems and give direction to solve them on the spot.
- For convenience of people, now days are allotted for different departments for dealing with problems of people. The prescribed day of a department like that of education, health, police and Home and others are advertised well in advance for the convenience of mass and minister, and officials of the concerned dapartment have been mandated to be present on the alloted day.

- A separate team of officials have been constituted to look after the letters handed over to the CM by the mass and they write the complaints about progress of work. Thousands of people from different parts of the state participate in the programme. Every petition is registered and given a number using which the status of the action taken on the case could be traced.
- The CM sits from 9 am to 5 pm hearing people's problems himself in a large hall which Lalu and Rabri used as fodder store for their cattle and poultry. The shed is waterproof and every visitor is provided a chair synonimous of one's dignified place in this humour world. The sitting arrangement is vast and around 2500 people could be accomodated in it at a time. The space has been expanded recently and the sitting capacity has been doubled, a development which reflects growing popularity of the event.
- District officers are given separate IDs and passwords to access the cases pertaining to their district brought before the CM at the programme. The programme has given confidence to citizens that they could directly approach the CM for their problem and it is a reminder for the officials that they could be pulled up anytime for their acts of omission and commission.
- The Janata Ke Darbar Mein Mukhyamantri programme also serves as an occasion for common man to interact with the CM directly. There had been occasion when people particularly women carry prasad for the CM (so dignified in himself to be so) which they have gathered from some temple. There are moments when somebody would bring a photograph of the CM reminding him of his old days which are accepted. On one occasion a youth came with *Nitish Chalisa* in the programme similar to *Lalu chalisa* of old times singing praise of the leaders and portraying them as hopes of the people. The youth who had brought *Nitish Chalisa* could not impress the CM who said, instead of wasting time in doing such thing he should concentrate on his studies and do better for himself and the society.
- On one such occasion, a group of teachers of *Madarsa* from some far off place had visited the CM with the

complaint that they have not been paid salary ahead of some festive occasion. The CM from the programme site itself telephoned the concerned officers to ensure that they get salary before the festival. The visitors many of whom were women returned with a big smile on their faces.

- The *Janata Darbar* is not restricted to the Chief Minister. Deputy Chief Minister Sushil Kumar Modi also holds similar programme. Even district magistrates and other field officers are holding similar sittings with the benefit of masses.
- Considering beneficial results of such a function many states have adopted it. Akhilesh Yadav, the young Chief Minister of neighbouring Uttar Pradesh is meeting common citizens on similar initiative. Himachal Pradesh CM Prem Kumar Dhumal also used to meet people at his residence in Shimla with spot-redress.
- To make himself more accessible for common citizens, Nitish has started writing blog joining the growing Indian blogging community comprising celebrities, politicians, professionals and many more.
- *Nitishspeaks.blogspot.com* can be logged on to see his personal views on schemes. In his first blog Nitish wrote about the popular cycle scheme his government is running for students, both boys and girls, of standard IX and above. He wrote "This, in fact, is an affirmation of the fact that a small initiative can really go a long way in bringing about a big change."
- On starting blogs, Nitish said it an attempt to reach out to more and more people's, within the country and beyond.
- The effort has been paying off, as the CM is receiving reactions from citizens within the state and abroad.
- Ramprawesh Puri—Chanaway thana—Thaway District Gopalganj writes, "*maa Kamakhaya ka aashorwad sada aap par bani rahe taki aap unki kripa se aanewale 20 baras (years) me Bihar hi nahi Bharat ko bhi apka netritwa (leadership) mil sake. Yadi aap dalit-mahadalit ke sath Goswami bandhuon (Giri, Puri, Bharti, Parbat etc) ko bhi pratinidhitwa dekar samtamu ithihas ka nayak bane. Bishes*

Bharat ki Janata aap ke taraf ash lagaye baithi hai.

- Zafrul Islam from Aurangabad district of Bihar writes, "Sir this is really a great work of development and crime deduction that you have done in Bihar. Every *Bihari* is proud to be called *Bihari* in place of feeling shame to say themselves a *Bihari*. But it needs more development in Bihar that is electricity and establishement of industries so that nobody could go out of the state. There is IT industry also necessary in Bihar. Thanks a lot Sir."
- Raghubar Singh presently living in Kolkata and who hails from Bihar's Buxar district writes, "Sir, *mai Bihar ke Buxar district ka rhne wala hun, aap per ham Bihar wasiyon ko garva hai, mai chhuttee me gaon gaya tha, kuch baten sunne ko mila jo mai apko awagat kara raha hoon, mnrega ke bisaya mei batana chahta hun jo hame gaon me gari ahul hai, mai asha karata hun ki aap mere gaon me ek bar jakar garibo ka halchal ki jankari len, hamari pancayat ka nam hai gayaghat.*"
- S.B. Singh—Ambala Cantt—a government employee writes, "Thanks for giving us pride to be called *Bihari*, otherwise it was an abuse. Now it gives us immense pleasure when our CM is appreciated even at world level. Please pay some attention towards schools in villages otherwise people are plying towards urban areas just to get their child basically educated. They think that these schools are made for some people who take payments free of cost and enjoy the lives well-respected as teacher. If required I shall give the proof."
- Mohammad Tanweer Irshad from Lahan Dhaka in Bangladesh writes, "We know that you have path of changing Bihar. But you have to control on *bhrashtrachar* (corruption) starting from top to bottom (panchayat level); do you think at panchayat level how many low level working staff are having 5-10 lacss cost four wheelers? Just enquire through each and every DTO of district, amazed you can think then the level of corruption existing at top level."
- To facilitate more interaction with the citizens directly and to provide occasion to people who could not come to

the state capital for *Janata ke darbar me Mukhya Mantri, Nitish is embarking on different yatras namely sewa yatra, pravas* and *viswas yatra* to come face-to-face with the local residents and improve social services delivery system.

- Under *Pravas Yatra* the CM and his entourage resides in a district for days to monitor progress of development works and interact with people to know the problems from horse mouth. The entire cabinet and senior officials accompany the CM on this *yatra* which symbolises bringing the government at the doorsteps of the people in different parts of the state. Nitish says during the programme he never misses to visit some estalishment concerned with agriculture to ensure faster growth of farm sector across the state.
- *Seva Yatra* has also been initiated on similar lines as part of which the CM moves around in the state to have first hand knowledge of effective implementation of the welfare schemes started by his government.The concept has been a great success among the on looking mass.

6

Challenges Ahead

- There is no denying the fact that Bihar has undergone a major transformation in recent times and has earned a good name for itself within the state and outside. But, many people thinks that these changes look big only when seen on the mirky seven of Lalu's dark days aboutm half-a-decade back.
- The growth seen in Bihar remains skewed and uneven, limited to trade, hotels, construction and communication. To make this development durable, the state needs to build robust material as well as abstract infrastructure that may bring heavy real transformation in the living standard of people and investment from outside.
- Planning Commision member Abhijit Sen had recently during Bihar global summit termed this as "Nursery and catchment area" growth and hence not sustainable and satisfactory.
- Chairman of the Aditya Birla group Kumar Mangalam Birla had in the same summit at Patna in February 2012 had said that heavy industry captains are hesitant to invest in Bihar without proper electricity supply.
- The growth story the Nitish Kumar government has been propagating is hinged largely on a comparison with the non-performance of its RJD predecessor.
- The successive RJD governments spent only Rs. 25,000 crore in 15 years, a figure the current government like to compare with the Rs. 28,000 crore budget for 2012-13 alone.

- But it is; when the government extends the comparison to states such as Gujarat and Maharashtra, it finds itself challenged strongly by experts.
- Sen attributed the growth to a boom in telecommunication and construction sectors. For the primary sector (agriculture, animal husbandry, forestry, mining and *quandary*) it has been a roller coaster ride with average growth fluctuating from minus 7.5 per cent in 2005-06 to 24.3 per cent in 2006-07, minus 6.2 per cent in 2007-08, 11 in 2008-09, minus 8.2 per cent in 2009-10 and 6.3 per cent in 2010-11.
- It is the secondary and tertiary sectors that have grown, Sen explained. Bihar has grown 11.3 per cent annually in the last few years, peaking at 14.8 per cent in 2010-11 but that year the secondary sector averaged only 6.3 per cent to the secondary sector's 19.2.
- Construction for example grew 26.1 per cent in 2010-11. With investors confidence boosted by the improvement in law and order, growth of the sector has been steady since the 24.1 per cent of 2005-06. But, this has been mostly Patna-centric with the last six years having seen over 10,000 apartments built and taking construction nearly to saturation point with few residential plots now available in liveable localities.
- Then Nitish complained that Sen was only "finding fault and not suggesting ways out". The government's own officials have meticulously compiled figures about what is wrong with Bihar.
- The Planning and Development department's presentation, "Bihar: A case for special category status" shows how per capita income has dropped consistently since the first Five year Plan period (1951-56) when it was Rs. 4,707 against a national average of Rs. 6,858, the gap being between 30 and 35 per cent. By the 10th Plan period (2002-07), it had shot up to 67.7. In the 11th Plan period it is 60.27 per cent.
- The government admits there is no major industry in Bihar. Of a total 14,55,321 industries in India, Bihar had only 1,774 (1.14 per cent) in 2008-09. About Bihar's power shortage, it says, the per capita power consumption level is 778 units.

- On the human development index, Bihar is at the bottom of the list with 0.049 in 2011, despite the government having started over two dozen welfare schemes for women, Scheduled Castes and Minorities.
- Compared to the 11 states already enjoying special category status, Bihar has the highest concentration of people living below the poverty line. The centre accepts 65 lacs as number of BPL families in Bihar, while the government estimates it as many as 1.45 crore people under BPL category.
- Another major problem on way to development hovers the corruption sneaking everywhere into the implementation of social services schemes.
- The government faced two major controversies. These were allocations of industrial plots under BIADA (Bihar Industrial Development Area) scheme. It has been alleged that many bureaucrats, ministers and legislators cornered for their relatives at subsidised rates through foul means. The more recent one is distribution of land under the Mahadalits Vikas Yojna to give 1.306.8 square feet plots to landless *mahadalit* families to build a home under the Indira Gandhi Awas Yojna.
- Reports suggested that in Araria, government officials and brokers ganged up to buy land dirt-cheap from villagers and sell the same to the government at four to five times higher prices.
- Besides, many beneficiaries who have got plots are still stranded due to lack of easements nor the house that the *yojna*, a showpiece scheme of the Nitish government, promises to deliver. In the Chief Minister's home district of Nalanda, several families have been alloted plots that fall in a 6.99 acre pond.
- Another major question looming large over continuation of the JD(U)-BJP government is about its survival in case the BJP decides to project Gujarat Chief Minister Narendra Modi as its Prime Ministerial candidate in 2014 general elections.
- Speculations are strong that Nitish might play a Naveen Patnaik in such a situation. In the wake of Kandamahal

controversy which arose due to murder of a RSS leader, the Biju Janata Dal (BJD) dumped BJP in the last assembly election and rode back to power in Orissa alone.

- Nitish Kumar who has carved out a strong constituency for himself and his JD (U) among minority after welcoming them away from Lalu's RJD has from the beginning made it clear that he can not compromise on the issue of Modi facing taint of Gujarat communal riots 2002.
- Bowing to Nitish dictat, the BJP did not field Narendra Modi to campaign for BJP candidates either in 2005 assembly elections or the one in November 2010. During BJP National Executive meeting at Patna in 2011, when advertisements came out in local newspapers about Narendra Modi contributing in rehabilitation of victims of Koshi floods, Nitish cancelled a dinner he had announced for the BJP leaders including its top brass L K Advani, Sushma Swaraj, Arun Jaitely and party chief Nitin Gadkari.
- Nitish had to face difficulties explaining to the people over the accidental handshakes he had with Narendra Modi, first during an NDA rally at Ludhiana during general elections in 2009 and the second one more recently during a meeting of Chief Ministers on NTRC. On both occasions, Modi walked up to Nitish to shake hand with him.
- RJD chief Lalu Prasad and LJP President Ramvilas Paswan lost no time in attacking Nitish for handshakes with Modi. Nitish managed to convince people that it was just part of a courtsey and his aversion for Modi has not changed.
- If Nitish who could also be an NDA candidate in 2014 due to his strong secular image decides to snap ties with the BJP, there could be no immediate threat to his government, as his party has 107 MLAs and he could muster the required number to reach a magic figure of 122 in the 243 member Bihar assembly with the help of Independents and others but would face a major problem in urban areas where its ally BJP has big mass bases.
- The two coalition partners witnessed unpleasant moments following remarks of BJP leader and Gujarat Chief Minister Narendra Modi that "casteist" leaders had pushed Bihar to economic backwardness. The comments made by Modi at

BJP's Gujarat state committee meeting at Rajkot in June 2012 attracted sharp reaction from Bihar Chief Minister Nitish Kumar, whose differences with Modi defies secret.

- In a pointed reply to Modi, Kumar said it was like "pot calling kettle back".
- Kumar said that Modi, who has been a constant irritant in the JD(U)-BJP coalition ties in Bihar, should mind his own business instead of making comments on others.
- "One should think about one's own situation while commenting on Bihar" (*Bihar per tippani karne waalon ko apni halaat ke bare mein sochna chaahiye*)" Nitish reacted to the Gujarat counterpart.
- He rejected Modi's contention about backwardness and the lack of development in Bihar and said the state has been marching on the path of development by taking care of various adversaries and problems besieging it over the years. "Bihar has been a place of learning since ancient times," Kumar said highlighting rich heritage of the state.
- Joining Nitish in attacking Modi, JD (U) president Sharad Yadav said that casteism exists in Gujarat also like other parts of the country. Yadav, who is convenor of NDA, said Gujarat is not ahead (in development) because of any individual, but it is ahead due to its geographical location.
- "Gujarat is not ahead because of any individual but due to its geographical location. Gujarat has not developed today but it was also developing during the British period like all other cities on the seashores.
- "People have a poor understanding of history and hence talking to it in their own way for temporary gains, but caste is a reality. Is Gujarat casteless? Which part of the country is out of caste influence?" Yadav asked.
- Seeing the issue taking a dangerous turn in relationship between the two coalition partners, Bihar's Deputy Chief Minister Sushil Kumar Modi gave a twist to the matter saying Gujarat Chief Minister's casteist remark was actually aimed at the previous RJD rule in Bihar during which the state had slipped to backwardness due to negative casteism being a factor.

- Though the matter died a slow death with both the parties exercising restraints, it signalled another round of spat between the two powerful Chief Ministers of the NDA—Narendra Modi and Nitish Kumar—who are considered as the opposition coalition's best bet for the 2014 general elections.
- The episode gave a stick to Nitish rivals like Lalu Prasad and Ramvilas Paswan to beat him saying since JD(U) is bending before the communal BJP, Bihar has to face such embarassing moments.
- Some day ago, Narendra Modi had created problem for Nitish Kumar for the second time by walking over to him during a conference of Chief Ministers over the issue of NCTC (National Counter Terrorism Committee) in Delhi and shaking hand with him. He had done a similar act during NDA's rally at Ludhiana during last general elections in 2009. Nitish had to convince his supporters particularly those from minority muslim community that there was no change of heart towards Modi, blamed for Gujarat communal riots of 2002.
- Besides these political events putting question marks round the longevity of JD(U)-BJP coalition government in Bihar since November 2005, there is serious debate whether the talks of development in Bihar is "real" or a "myth."
- A leading English magazine had recently in its cover page story raised the question. It differentiated between myth and reality about Bihar on six count and highlighted that Bihar's growth story and making a lofty reputation for the Chief Minister have been a smart work done by some "spin doctors" working in his favour.
- Giving points and counterpoints, the write up differentiated between the reality and the myth.
- Talking about the first myth that Bihar became the fastest growing state in the shortest possible time, it said Bihar had clocked double digit growth rate in the 1990s, fluctuating wildly; growth numbers mean little when starting from zero or negative growth.
- Secondly, about agriculture policies being progressive in Bihar now, it said agriculture's share in the state's GDP

is declining, though 87 per cent of the population lives in rural areas. Reforms such as dismantling APMC (Agriculture Produce Marketing Committee) as done in Darbhanga have been a disaster fuelling food inflation.

- Against the contention of Bihar being a safe place to do business, it says the reality is that a certain kind of state-sponsored criminal is much diminished. Yet, gains are being lost as other crimes like burglaries, theft, kidnapping and rape continue.
- The myth that Bihar will be a dynamic industrial state soon, has the reality vedrsion that investments are only trickling into this land-locked, agrarian state that is beset by floods for four months in a year.
- Next, Bihar's consumer economy is rich with possibilities. The reality is that per capita income has grown (though not in farms). Inflation is high, too. Bihar's bank branches are just 5 per cent of the country's share, leaving little scope for credit growth.
- The last and sixth myth is that Bihar is building roads at breckneck speed, but critics say it's true, roads, bridges and homes are being built but they're not engines in a state where micro enterprises dominate.
- The critics says Nitish's growth is "*chimera*", the result of an overly critical eye on the previous regime's failings. They compare the last four years of Lalu's time when growth averaged 5.87 per cent with Nitish's first four years of 6.35 per cent growth, and see no miracle.
- Talking about the so called growth process, the critics say share of agriculture in Bihar's GDP has declined from 42 to roughly 20 per cent and the farm incomes fell alongside three years of negative agricultural growth. So what explains the growth pattern of Bihar?
- Even a cursory look around cities like Patna, Ara, Buxar, Hajipur, Samastipur and Darbhanga show palpable changes in last seven years. The changes are visible from the point of view of opening of more restaurants to satiate the needs of families who prefer to have food outside sometime particularly on weekends which could afford due to improved law and order situation. Data shows that

restaurants and trading—an employment intensive business—grew nearly 30 per cent over 2008-11.

- Real estate business continues to flourish particularly in the capital town of Patna where citizens are preferring to have property developed in a swanky style at their old sites. The construction sector has witnessed a growth of 10 per cent since 2008 (and over 13 per cent in 2011 against a mere 4 per cent in 2004). Bihar also had the highest off take of cements in India in 2011 and this boom rides residential demand more than anything else, supplied by the ubiquitous brick-kiln springing up across the rural landscape—the only apparent sign of industrialisation.
- Since 2006, registered vehicles have grown 50-fold in Bihar from around 80,000 to 3.87 lacs by 2011.
- Notwithstanding visits of several industrialists, industrial investments coming to Bihar is still miniscule. A diamond unit assuring Rs. 500 crore investment besides enquiries by Pepsi, Godrej, Max, Nestle, Britainia and HUL, Bharti company chiefs nothing concrete has arrived on the ground so far yet.
- A FICCI study with Konrad Adeneur foundation in December 2011 found none of the Rs. 42,491 crore investment approved by June 2011 was implemented. Only Rs. 62 crore of the Rs. 93,577 crore approved since 2008 saw the light of the day.
- In 2008, industry was a mere 3.8 per cent of Bihar's GDP as compared to 20 per cent of national level.
- Four sectors—communications, trade, hotels and manufacturing and construction—grew at over 15 per cent from 2004 to 2011. Since 2005-06, Bihar has added more than four crore phone connections.
- The critics say whatever betterment has taken place in Bihar in recent years has been mainly due to liberal finance provided by the Centre. They say Bihar depends excessively on central grants to meet expenses. Debt is spiralling. The CAG has revealed that Nitish's bureaucrats are not spending effectively as ever. For 99 schemes in 2011, bulk of expenses were drawn on the last day of the financial year.

- Actually, grants from the Centre, which grew six-fold to Rs. 24,000 crore in 2011, could be the real secret of Bihar's growth, and not agriculture, not enterpreunership, not even services. Nitish decision to support Pranab Mukherjee in Presidential election paid handsome monetary assistance from the Centre. The Planning Commission has enhanced budgetary allocation for Bihar to 28,000 crore, up by almost 30 per cent as compared to last year. It also provided it a special assistance of Rs. 2000 crore for five years that comes to Rs. 400 crore for each year in the 12th Five Year plan (2012-17).
- Comparing Bihar with other states highlights some glaring facts. Bihar's per capita plan outlay is Rs. 1,931 compared to Gujarat's Rs. 4,645, Haryana's Rs. 4,743 and Karnataka's Rs. 5,594.
- Even when compared to the 11 states already enjoying special status, Bihar has the highest concentration of people living below poverty line. The Centre accepts 65 lacs as the number of BPL families in Bihar to whom they provide subsidised ration but as per the state government's count the number of BPL families is as high as 1.45 crore.
- Though the debate between the claims of development and reality is going on, one thing is pretty visible that Bihar is witnessing a change. Free from fear of crimes, citizens are enjoying a better life style and standard. Opening of NIT and Chanakya Law College in Patna means more and more students from outside coming to the state for higher studies, something which was not there earlier.
- There is no denying the fact that Bihar has embarked on a different journey.

PHOTOGRAPHS

Milk Men Packaging Milk at Sudha, the Bihar Version of Amul Dairy.

Bunch of Girls Pedalling to School.

Chief Minister Nitish Kumar Planting Sapling of Bodhi Tree at his One Anne Marg Residence in Patna.

Smiling Girls Present Flowers to Chief Minister Nitish Kumar at a School in Bihar.

School Girls Spreading Strong Social Message in Interior Areas of Bihar.

Tasty Sudha Peda (Sweet) Symbolising Sweetness of Bihar Progress.

A New Look Primary School in Bihar.

Refurbished Secondary Girls School at Koilwar in Bhojpur District of Bihar Symbolising the Message of Strong School Infrastructure.

Chief Minister Nitish Kumar in Company of his Deputy Sushil Kumar Modi Inaugurating Makhana Brand.

Chief Minister Nitish Kumar in a Makhana Factory to See How the Wheel of Growth is Moving in Bihar.

A Shining Road in a Village in Bihar.

A Road Construction in Progress in an Interior Area in Bihar.

Villages Linked Through Concrete Roads in Bihar

Smoke Billows from Chimney of Closed Harinagar Sugar Mill in West Champaran District Again in Nitish Raj.

Sugarcane Loaded Tractors Rushing to Harinagar Sugar Mill which has come in Action After a Long Time in Nitish Raj.

Road Construction Work in Progress in a Bihar Village.

Workers Busy in Building a Road on a Way to Prosperity in a Village.

Path to Progress: Four lane N.H 57 Ram Nagar, Araria in Bihar.

Nitish Watches a Weaver Spinning Yarn.

An Overbridge Bathing in Floodlight in Patna Reflecting Transformation of the State in Nitish Raj.

Chief Minister Nitish Kumar at Inauguration of Chanakya Law University at Patna.

Fast Tracking Road Traffic in Patna.

Free from Fear People Take a Walk in a Park in Late Evening in Patna.

Buddha Smriti in Patna Built at the Ruins of Old Jail Building that was Inaugurated by the Dalai Lama Show Shining the New Glory of Bihar.

Foreigners Rubbing Shoulder with Native Indians at Buddha Smriti Park in Patna, the New Symbol of Bihar Progress.

A Busy Dak Bunglow Roundabout in Patna Showing Busy Life of People.

Girls Engrossed in Study in a Bihar Government School.

A Colourful Evening at a Park in Patna Symbolising Happy Times in Bihar During Nitish Raj.

Pillar of Strength: Mahatma Gandhi Setu at Patna on River Ganga.

Muslim Girls Busy in Books at a School in Bihar.

Minority Muslim Welfare in Mind: Nitish at a Hunar (Vocational Course) Centre for Muslim Women.

Patna Wears a New Look in Nitish Raj.

Magardehi Bridge on Budhi Gandak (Darbhanga-Samastipur).

Women Empowerment :
A Woman Busy in her Agriculture Field.

Nrega Work in Progress in Bihar.

Women Busy in a Nrega Work in Bihar.

Walking Along for Bihar Progress: APJ Abdul Kalam with Nitish Kumar.

Nitish Sharing Thoughts with Missle Man APJ Abdul Kalam on Bihar Growth.

Pranab Mukherjee Congratulating Nitish.

Nitish Kumar with Vice President Hamid Ansari.

Uneasy Handshake between Nitish and Narendra Modi.

Friendly Gesture of Nitish and Narendra Modi Hiding Uncomfortable Relationship between them.

Show of Strength: Nitish with Vajpayee and L.K. Advani

Powerful Equation : Nitish with Advani.

Deep in Conversation Nitish with Bihari Babu.

Uncomfortable Handshake:
Nitish with Lalu and Ramvilas Paswan.

Nitish with Prime Minister Manmohan Singh.

Index